MONEY, FAMILY, SEX & HAPPINESS

MONEY, FAMILY, SEX & HAPPINESS

HOW TO CREATE A LIFE OF DEEP MEANING AND FULLFILMENT

Barbara Longué

Money, Family, Sex & Happiness
You Can Have it All
Copyright © 2019 by Barbara Longué

All rights reserved. No part of this book may be reproduced, stored in a retrieval system, or transmitted in any form or by any means – electronic, mechanical, photocopy, recording, scanning, or other, – except for brief quotations in critical reviews or articles, without the prior written permission of the publisher.

Published in Tasmania, Australia by Vortex Publishing
215 Dalmayne Road
Gray TAS 7215
Australia

Contact the Publisher:
Phone: +61 0448516488
Email: blongue@gmail.com

ISBN: 978-0-6484639-4-8 BL (AU)
978-0-6484639-3-1 BL (US)
Cover and Interior Design by Joy Fluckiger

Table of Contents

Foreword vii
Introduction ix

PART I: Is There More To Life? Or What the Hell Happened? 1

Chapter 1: Pneumonia Body & Soul 2
Chapter 2: Flashback 7
Chapter 3: Coney Island Crazy 10
Chapter 4: Quitting the Dream 15
Chapter 5: Awakening in Machu Picchu 21
Chapter 6: Meditation Visions 28
Chapter 7: Goodbye Milou 32
Chapter 8: The Split 35
Chapter 9: Hurricane Sandy 39
Chapter 10: Time To Move 45
Chapter 11: Sell The House 49

PART II: My Tassie Life 55

Chapter 12: Life Down Under 56
Chapter 13: Tassie Dreams 58
Chapter 14: Losing My Identity 63
Chapter 15: Leaving Family Behind 67
Chapter 16: I Get Paid For That Now 71

Chapter 17: Internet Addiction 74
Chapter 18: Am I Living In A Cave? 78
Chapter 19: Aussie, Aussie, Aussie 83
Chapter 20: Volunteers 86
Chapter 21: Dunneys or Longdrops…Hmmm 92
Chapter 22: The Laurel Tree 96
Chapter 23: Every Time, It's a Miracle 99
Chapter 24: Mom's Dementia 105
Chapter 25: Sleepless Nights 111
Chapter 26: Struggle In Paradise 117

PART III: Your Highest Self 125
Chapter 27: What's Next? 126
Chapter 28: A New Beginning 128
Chapter 29: Case Study 133
Chapter 30: Lies and More Lies 139
Chapter 31: What is the Meaning Behind That? 144
Chapter 32: It's An Inside Job 151
Chapter 33: Mindfulness 155
Chapter 34: Gratitude Porn 160
Chapter 35: Time Abundance 165
Chapter 36: Choose Yourself First 171
Chapter 37: Create Your Day 176
Chapter 38: Awakened Profitability Coaching 183
    Afterword 185
    Appendix and Contact Information 188
    Acknowledgments 189
    About the Author 190

Foreword

Each of us takes many journeys in our lives. Sometimes we hike up the hillside in a nearby park. Sometimes we plan a big trip to another continent. Both can be a lot of fun and create memories.

Other journeys we take can be inside. Journeys that don't even involve moving anywhere. Emotional or spiritual journeys that can be difficult or easy, thoughtful or fearful, pleasant or soul stretching.

Spending time understanding our journeys is a rewarding and powerful experience.

However, most of the time, we rarely take the time to reflect and ponder and gather the obvious fruit and powerful nuance that is available from these exploratory processes.

Barbara has candidly and deeply explored her heart as she shares with us major life transitions, major geographic relocations, and life-changing discoveries that have propelled her for the last few years.

Over the last few years, my acquaintance and friendship with Barbara have been joyful, powerful, and heart changing.

Watching her and helping her and listening as she discovers the old, the new and the profound has been a wonderful treat.

Wherever you are on your life's journey if you want to connect powerfully and make meaning from your past, discover your future and mine the purpose from the journeys you have already experienced, and those that lie ahead of you in the blank pages of your future, Barbara's book will be a worthy and joyful companion.

Learning to consider your heart carefully, honestly examining your motives and learnings are all treasures you will unearth as you venture deep into your journeys.

Congratulations and deepest love to Barbara for sharing the glories of her life, explorations and rediscovered wisdom in this delightful volume.

Kellan Fluckiger

February 2019

Introduction

Physically moving from one side of the world to the other is a daunting and courageous undertaking. By making such a decision, I mistakenly assumed I was home free, or at least close.

Through the months and years that followed, I had to get used to a lot of new things. There was the strange accent, different foods, laid-back lifestyle, and a hundred other things.

However, nothing was anywhere near as difficult as the emotional upheaval that seemed to accompany every new thing. Somehow, despite the appeal and excitement, almost everything hooked into some memory of the past.

I had some feeling that I had failed, or had chosen poorly, in taking such a bold move in declaring my independence.

While life has regular ups and downs in New Jersey or Tasmania, I seemed to magnify everything through the lens of the emotional tsunami I had unleashed with my life-changing decision.

"You can stop being the biggest block to your success by creating your habits and meaningful desires."

— Barbara Longué

PART I:

Is There More To Life? Or What the Hell Happened?

CHAPTER 1

Pneumonia Body & Soul

I was dazed and confused and wasn't even sure where I was.

Slowly, through the fog in my mind and the pain in my body, I started to remember a few things. I recognized the walls of the room I was in and the painting my daughter made when she was four.

That meant I was home and in bed. Wow, it had been four days, and my temperature was still 104°F. Delirium, where I faded in and out of reality, had become commonplace.

My attention drifted back to the painting. When she created it, I thought she was a genius and the most talented four-year-old ever! I smiled through the pain and the massive pounding headache echoing through my ears as I realized that every parent must think the same thing.

I returned an hour earlier from the doctor's office, my second trip that week. I was grateful to finally have a diagnosis that explained why I couldn't move, couldn't breathe and couldn't walk without help.

Pneumonia. Great, just great. The doctor prescribed a more powerful antibiotic than the one I had gotten a few days before.

I had decided that after three days of no improvement from the first medication, I just had to do something different. So, back to the doctor, I went.

I'm sure the drive was only a few minutes, as it was only a half mile from my house, but it seemed like forever. I waited for x-rays. I waited for explanations. I think I waited just to be waiting, but eventually, I got some answers.

The nurse called the pharmacy so that the medication would be ready faster. The doctor was convinced I should be admitted into a hospital. There was simply no way I was going to do that. No way at all.

It was something that I had even gone to the doctor. I never went to doctors unless I was nearly dead. Given that I felt that way at that moment, I guess a doctor visit was in order. The elephant sitting on my chest was keeping me from breathing, and it became increasingly evident that the elephant wasn't going anywhere.

I don't remember the drive home. I remember the pain I felt getting into the car after I left the doctor's office and something about squinting and trying to keep it together on the drive.

Even though it was only half a mile, it was an ordeal. Getting out of the car at home was just as awful. I staggered into the house.

Knowing there was no way I could make another trip that day, today I called my friend Maria to pick up my prescription. She agreed, and soon, the doorbell rang. I stumbled out of bed as the front door opened, and I heard Maria step into the kitchen.

I fell asleep hoping that the antibiotics would do the trick to get me up and about quickly. I wasn't used to being sick and feeling helpless, lost, and completely lacking control of my life.

Thankfully, within 48 hours of taking the new medication, my temperature dropped to 100ºF, and I was able to shuffle my way from the bed to the living room to watch an endless stream of movies.

My husband and kids struggled valiantly on their own to fend for themselves, cooking and cleaning. I felt bad that I couldn't do the things I was supposed to be doing.

Although I felt guilty of my incapacitation over the next three weeks, I was glad for the much-needed rest. I caught up on every Sopranos episode starting from the beginning. I was binge watching DVDs from the library long before binge streaming was popular.

We hadn't had cable TV in our house in over ten years. There was no local television station, so we relied on Blockbuster and the local library for movies. Imagine my excitement when I found a new service called Netflix willing to send out three DVDs at a time.

Funny to reflect on how archaic that sounds in today's world of streaming TV, but that was my reality.

I was living on chicken soup, and as much bed rest as I could get. The days turned into weeks, and I still found myself incredibly weak and barely able to walk.

I was learning to feel less guilty about asking for help, particularly getting back and forth to the doctor's office. The incredible coughing fits were still quite a challenge.

I was astonished how hard it was to ask for help from anyone; for any reason, it seemed. Somehow it was not okay. Whether the help was from a doctor, my husband, my kids, my friends, or anyone else, it brought up sensations of weakness and guilt.

My internal story was, "It's bad to be weak." I guess I thought I was strong and in control.

That feeling of an incredible need to be self-sufficient had also turned me into a workaholic and a control freak. Lying in stillness would've been sheer torture if it weren't for the fact that I literally couldn't move.

On the fourth week, I went back to the doctor for another chest x-ray, and he declared my pneumonia healed.

The problem was, I still couldn't walk and breathe at the same time. I asked, "How is it possible that my pneumonia is healed if I can't walk and breathe at the same time?"

The doctors' medical wisdom explained that I just needed to be patient. My supply of patience had long since been exhausted. This was ridiculous!

Now I was getting angry. I had done everything the doctor said:

> Rest.
> Drink plenty of fluids.
> More rest.

While it was a massive improvement that I was able to breathe easier if I sat or lay still, it was that damn walking and breathing at the same time that I was incapable of doing.

My legs moved, but I could only take one or two steps at a time before I had to stop, rest, and catch my breath. That didn't seem like recovering from pneumonia to me.

I was so done with the invalid act. I told the doctor I wanted to see a specialist. They must have a breathing specialist somewhere, I reasoned.

He said I had a couple of choices. I could relax and rest, or go on another four-week course of massive antibiotics.

I knew how damaging long-term antibiotics usage could be to the health of the overall body health, and I didn't want that.

I left the doctor's office, thoroughly dejected, angry, and frustrated. I had no clue what to do next. I had already been more than patient.

I wanted to get back to my life.

CHAPTER 2

Flashback

As I reflected on the whole messy journey, I remembered certain events.

I was having lunch at Alba Vineyards in New Jersey with the Society of Wine Educators when I suddenly had the feeling that something was terribly wrong.

This was an important lunch, and we had brought a group of consumers and wine enthusiasts to the winery to get a glimpse of what happens at crush, (harvest time) in the wine industry.

It no longer mattered because I knew I had to get home. I didn't know what it was, just that I had to leave right then.

My head ached when I stood up. We were in the middle of the main course, and I just stood up, mumbled an excuse, and began the hour and a half drive home.

I was extremely anxious that something had happened with the kids. What had started as a mild headache at lunch was now throbbing. By the time I reached the kids on the phone, I was panicked.

They said everything was OK. They were both at home, and everything was as it should be. Relieved on that front, I thought about what I should do. I was already halfway home, and my headache was now a huge problem, so I kept driving.

By the time I pulled over to a gas station to buy some aspirin, I had thought my head would explode. It was all I could do to maintain my composure to stay focused on the road for the remaining thirty minutes or so.

Completely collapsing into the bed, I thought a short nap would make it all go back to normal. However, when I woke up hours later, I was completely exhausted and unable to do anything but lay in bed and rest.

As usual, I thought, a good night's sleep would make everything okay. I was sure I would be back to normal in the morning.

The next morning, not only was I not better, but I had a raging fever of 102°F. My extreme and sudden illness overcame my usual reluctance to go to the doctor. Thankfully, the local urgent care doctor in town was able to see me and gave me antibiotics for what they termed "nasal congestion and coughing."

I was still quite hopeful that everything would be fine after one more day, so I resigned myself to another 24 hours of absolute rest.

I vaguely remembered something about the winery tour the previous day. I had a flash of remembering the winemaker, demonstrating how to inoculate the tank with yeast. I watched him dump out and swirl in two pounds of yeast into the vat to kickstart the fermentation.

I remembered noticing that the mist of yeast had sprayed up and made a giant cloud around the top of the tank as the winemaker stirred the yeast into the mix. Then, how suddenly the headache, the body aches, and fever had come on.

Still, I was a bit relieved to have a day off work. My regular schedule had me working 60 to 80 hours per week, as well as trying to be at home most nights, making dinner for my family.

Having business events on the weekend was becoming an increasing problem. It seemed to require nearly all of my nights and weekends in addition to the standard 9-to-5 job. It was more like an 8 a.m. to midnight job.

Somehow, I was living the supermom myth. In my head, I imagined that I could do everything and do it well. Instead, I was busy racing up and down the highway, meeting clients and forever hurrying to be at the next place.

I had handed over control of my life to everyone else. Because I never got everything done, I thought I had a time management problem. I merely needed to be able to do MORE stuff faster and better. Everything everybody needed was always a top priority because I thought it was my responsibility to get it all done.

I was always in a hurry, and there was no time for me. I'm sure my kids thought I hadn't spent enough time with them either! If I was feeling rushed, what were they feeling? Also, because of my compulsive nature, whenever I was with them, I was distracted, thinking about everything but them.

So a day in bed would be a relief if I could get rid of that massive headache.

CHAPTER 3

Coney Island Crazy

The cold December wind was freezing me to the bone despite the ski jacket, hat, and gloves. My inner critic was relentlessly beating the "you're-out-of-your-mind" drum so loudly that it was hard to think.

Thankfully, the 7:00 a.m. Sunday drive through Manhattan had been smooth, uncrowded, and uneventful in spite of the coughing fits that felt like my head could come off. As I walked toward the water on Coney Island, through a park covered in thick, packed snow, I realised that I was probably crazy.

Five weeks earlier, I was diagnosed with pneumonia. The doctor now pronounced me, "cured." This made no sense to me as I could barely walk and breathe at the same time. I struggled to remember what on earth made me think this early morning trip was a good idea when I should still be in bed.

My mind wandered back to the conversation I had with Fred Leighton, a good customer, and friend.

A few days earlier, when he heard I had pneumonia, he told me about a friend of his named Chet who did some version of martial arts and healing with "some guy in Coney Island."

It sounded crazy, but I was desperate to feel better. Feeling warm and dry at the time, I talked myself into showing up on the beach in Coney Island at 7 a.m. to see what this intriguing new martial arts approach could do for me especially since the drive was 90 minutes from the house.

The moment I hung up the phone with Chet, I knew I wouldn't be able to get up at 5:30 a.m. to make it by the start time. I didn't care if this new teacher had magic beans or potions, getting up that early wasn't going to happen.

I made a pact with myself to leave at a much more "reasonable" 6:30 a.m. The extra sleep didn't eliminate the coughing fits on the drive over. Once or twice I worried that I might lose control of my car and end up in somebody else's lane.

"At least I'm driving a tank," I consoled myself. Well, as close to a tank as I could get. The heavy Chrysler 300 was the company car, and I felt at least slightly relieved that the bulk would provide some degree of protection in a wreck. I had no idea what to expect, and my concern that this might be another wild goose chase was not particularly comforting.

My mind snapped back to the present as I arrived at the edge of the water. I saw half a dozen people of all shapes and sizes moving in strange ways, arms flying overhead with bodies twisting and twirling around.

I took in the strangeness of the scene for a moment and considered making a run for it to the safety of my car. Except I knew that I couldn't run at all and collapsing on the ground was not what I had in mind for the morning.

I was dragging my body forward to get to the group. Chet met me and introduced a man I would call Sifu. I had no idea how profound and lasting that introduction would be, or what was coming. For the next five years, I addressed this man as "Sifu," which means teacher.

Given the reference to martial arts, I was expecting to meet some strong little Chinese or Korean fellow with incredible power. This big black man I had just been introduced to was another surprise.

Sifu and I chatted for a bit to get acquainted. He then told me to walk very slowly and practice "qigong breathing." I didn't understand exactly what was happening, mainly because he was asking me to breathe differently than I had been for most of my life!

I think he gave up, at least for that moment, on trying to teach me how to breathe correctly and just had me do some slow walking. In the moments that followed, each time he came near me, he said I was going too fast.

"How was that possible?" I thought. In my pneumonia recovery mode, I felt like I could barely move. So my movements already seemed excruciatingly slow. I tried to play along, but it was hard.

My usual mode of operation was that I liked to do things fast. Quick. Get shit done. Drive fast. Eat fast. Quickly finish one thing and move onto something else.

So this agonizing dance in frozen molasses felt like torture. Trying to go even slower than my sick body would take me. Like a child on a long trip, I kept asking, "am I done yet?"

Since I'm being honest, I guess that means I had no patience either. This is one of the many discoveries that has come to me on this journey of mystery and magic.

My patience has improved a bit, not that most people would call me patient now, but back then? Somehow I had decided that impatience was a crowning achievement and I had carried it to a high art form, with myself and everyone around me.

Finally, he told me I could finish walking. He directed me to stand by a tree, gently put my hands on it and told me just to breathe.

This was a lot easier, or so I thought until the tears started to flow. It was bitterly cold, and the tears were freezing as they streamed down my face.

I had no idea why I was crying. I was angry, frustrated, and mad at the world. Mad at my body for letting me down. "Just keep breathing," said Sifu.

He continued, "control your breath, control your life." "Shit, what a crazy statement," my mind replied. I was hoping my thoughts weren't audible. "I came here because I couldn't breathe, and now you're telling me my life depends on it."

I realized I already knew what happens when you can't breathe. The tears slowed down, and I was glad that I was facing the tree. I was hoping that Sifu couldn't hear or see me crying, but I knew better. It didn't matter; I wanted to believe it anyway.

The entire process lasted about an hour, and I was exhausted. Surprisingly, I was able to easily walk back to the car and was starting to feel better.

By the time I reached home, my husband was in shock. He saw me walking without hunching over trying to grab something to catch my breath. Moreover, he saw a smile coming over my face, something he hadn't seen in over a month.

That one-hour was one of the most transformative of my life. After that day, there were many hours of Qigong training and practice with Sifu and other mentors.

I wasn't sure how it happened, but the sudden shift from being so sick I was dragging my body around, to being able to walk, talk and smile again was a shock, a wake-up call, and a blessing.

The question now was: "What am I going to do with this amazing renewed ability to walk, talk and breathe?"

CHAPTER 4

Quitting the Dream

What could be wrong with being a fine wine buyer, traveling all over the world, visiting the most amazing wineries on the planet, entertaining customers at the finest restaurants and discovering incredible artisan winemakers following their passion for making great wine?

Nothing. It was my dream job! My dream life! My husband had a prestigious position as head of the United Nations Radio Unit for the French language. I had two beautiful children who were the magic in my life.

I had a black Labrador whom I adored. I had the proverbial house with a white picket fence. There wasn't really a fence, but it felt like it. By any measure, it should have been my dream life.

I had no clue why I was still unhappy. I felt guilty because I wanted more out of my life. "What more could there be?" I wondered.

My friend Kevin Kelley told me I was burning the candle not just at both ends but also in the middle. I knew I was trying to do everything and be everything to everyone.

I had become a workaholic. I thought I knew what I wanted, and I was going to get it. I was Super-Mom. With time to think, I suddenly realised that I was no longer so sure.

It was clear that being a workaholic had nearly killed me. I knew that I was getting stronger physically, as I continued to practice Qigong. Something else was happening at the same time. As I dove deeper into this beautiful internal martial art of Breathwork, I was calling everything in my life into question.

I found a new doctor who did integrative medicine. For the first time, I began to find out what was going on in my body. It turned out I was being poisoned by heavy metals in my body, specifically arsenic.

This might have come from my workplace, or perhaps years earlier in the vineyards where I could have become contaminated by older pesticide sprays.

I had chelation therapy to eliminate the toxins and rebuild my immune system, Qigong breathwork to restore my damaged lungs, megavitamins to counter my body's gross vitamin deficiencies, a new water filter in the house and a new air filter.

Excited by my progress, each week, I found something new to test out to improve my mental and physical health. In the past, I had practised yoga with great success.

However, when the yoga centre refinished the floor, I couldn't attend classes there anymore. Something in the chemicals they used in the refinishing process triggered an allergic reaction, even six months after the refinishing.

Qigong was now my mantra. Every weekend I made the long drive back and forth to Coney Island to practice with my teacher. It seemed that every waking moment, I was busy proselytizing about the benefits of Qigong. I'm sure I bored everyone to tears talking about Qigong at every opportunity.

I loved my renewed health and vigor, but my returning health and strength didn't resolve my growing certainty that I wasn't happy, still not satisfied. Something was missing.

I didn't know what it was.

I knew that the clock kept ticking and years kept passing, especially as busy as I had made my life. I knew that my concept of being a Super-Mom and trying to do everything wasn't working.

I wanted to spend more time with my kids. I realised my daughter was growing up and would soon be a high school senior, while I was in a blur of motion, always racing forward to the next thing.

Six weeks in bed brought up more questions than answers. My body healed, but the guilt remained. In the years I had missed, important things had passed me by.

By traditional standards, I was successful. I had good friends. I had a good job and all the external signs of success. I now began wondering if the constant conflicts with my husband were normal or if there was something seriously wrong.

Each moment I spent choosing myself was a moment that added to the feeling that I didn't want to be working anymore. I was finally getting clarity on what I didn't want, even if I couldn't yet clearly express what I did want.

I didn't want to attend any more boring corporate meetings to show team solidarity. The challenges of my job left me overworked. Adding more sales and corporate meetings to show team support for projects that didn't involve me felt like a waste of time.

The only part of the business I enjoyed focusing on was the wine. My interest in wine started in college, developed through training be a winemaker in Burgundy and Bordeaux and had never wavered. Working for a liquor company with a fine wine division meant I had to pretend to be interested when a new vodka, gin, or whiskey came out. This added extra time to my workload and pulled me away from the part of the business I loved and time with my family.

Working out, doing martial arts training at least an hour each day, two to three hours on the weekend, was making me strong. Not just physically strong, but mentally and spiritually as well as.

When I added everything together, I knew I didn't want to work long hours anymore. I just hadn't figured out how to adjust my schedule or my job to make that happen.

One Sunday in June, as I was obsessing in my head over what was wrong with my life, I realised that my workaholic tendencies were compounded by working for a large corporation full of other workaholics – it all seemed so normal. After all, that appeared to be the standard requirement in so many professions and so many jobs.

It was a sunny day at the park in Coney Island, and I was doing a particularly challenging exercise, which made me sweat within the first two steps. The exercise consisted of a long slow walk, holding a form (pose) for 30 seconds before moving on slowly to the next step.

The assignment was to walk across the playground and back. It took me nearly 3 hours.

By the time I completed the exercise, I had realised I had to quit my job and do something else. There were three people I had in mind to call that day to see what this next step might bring.

By later that afternoon, I made all three calls and had commitments to work with them after leaving my job.

Done.

All that was left to do was resign. That turned out to be much harder than I had anticipated. I had been fortunate to work for one of the best individual owners of a large corporation I could imagine.

Richard Leventhal is a rare breed of entrepreneurs. He has utmost integrity in his relations with all of his suppliers and everyone that he does business with. I was so grateful for the opportunity to watch and learn from him.

He also had a great second in command, General Manager Neil Barnet. He was an incredible leader with an eagle eye on every detail in the organisation and was a great mentor to me.

Of course, because of how I felt about my loyalty to Richard and Neil, I felt guilty, just thinking about quitting my job.

Even though it was difficult, I took the leap, which meant I was officially retired--for the first time in my life.

I planned to create a new business, working only part-time in the upscale wine business as a brand manager and marketing consultant for wineries selling in the New York/New Jersey region.

I planned to keep that activity small so that I could spend a third of my time getting into real estate, and a third of my time in the stock market. It was August 2005, and I was excited about what the future might hold.

I could easily envision spending quality time with my kids and my husband, traveling as I wanted, working out as often as I wished to and enjoying life again. I wanted to stop all the chatter in my head and LIVE.

One powerful lesson I took away from working with Richard was to focus on the creation of partnerships with both vendors and customers. He believed that a successful business could be a win-win proposition. It was always about finding a way to make things work.

This lesson and many others guided me as I launched my new venture with high hopes for the future.

CHAPTER 5

Awakening in Machu Picchu

I was huffing and puffing as I reached the top of Huayna Picchu, the peak that towers over Machu Picchu. Oh, but what a view. The sweat was pouring off my forehead, and the water had the best taste after the 2-hour climb.

The early morning climb was a bit stressful because I needed to get to the "gates" before they closed off the number of climbers for the day. Every inch of the climb was interesting. Tiny orchids of incredible beauty and a refreshing, gentle breeze combined with frightening drops over the sides of cliffs kept the adrenaline on high.

The 5 a.m. start wasn't a problem. There wasn't even a line at the entrance. My anticipation was immense as I started the climb. In addition to water and snacks, my trusty backpack was a veritable catch-all full of handy things I might need that day. That backpack had seen me through many overseas trips.

The sun was coming up over the mountain as I began the climb to the top. I was in good shape at the time from my 2-hour daily workout, but heights were never my specialty. Combining that with the effects of the higher altitudes over the previous days, I became a bit unsteady climbing over the rocks and around the stone stairs that meandered their way up to the top.

I had come with a group of 11 other women and the trip leader, a man named Tyberon, or Tyb for short. This was our free day to explore Machu Picchu and let the energies of the place sink in.

All but a few of the members of the trip were making their way up the peak, and as I made my way up, we passed each other numerous times. The stairs down the mountain were far more frightening than the climb up, steep stairs with a 60-degree slope and no handrail.

The drop plummets down to the bottom of the valley nearly 2,720 metres. The view was awesome, but the potential for vertigo was present.

In preparation for this trip, our group had a few online meetings to introduce ourselves and connect. During those meetings, Tyb declared that we were all soul family on this trip and a month's preparation was vital to get the most out of this sacred journey.

When I had booked the trip, I was just looking to visit Machu Picchu. I had never heard anyone talk about mystical stuff like "soul family" or anything of the sort.

My husband had decided to go to Brazil to compete in another Ironman. This trip was at a time that presented a significant conflict with my wine business. So off he went on his adventure.

This created a negotiation, and as a result, I was given a free pass by my husband to book this trip of my dreams for my own private adventure.

A quick search on the internet had brought up Tyb's group trip to Peru.

The timing worked well, and as a bonus, I was able to convince my brother Tim to book the trip as well.

Tim pulled out the week before the start date. At that time, the Lehman Brothers crisis seemed imminent, and he was worried that those events would affect his business. He felt like he needed to be available at home.

Trips to Europe, especially France and Spain, were real highlights for me. My work provided for these trips to be a frequent opportunity. The kids and my husband Jerome spent 2-4 weeks in France every summer.

In the wine business, it was common for me to take one or two other trips every year to wine country in Europe. We were fortunate to have the money and time to take the kids on some fantastic holidays discovering the Mayan Peninsula in Mexico, the Costa Brava in Spain and Gaudi's famous architecture.

We also went hiking in Vermont, San Francisco, the Grand Canyon, and even Croatia and Bosnia Hercegovina about five years after the conclusion of their Civil War. We loved to travel as a family, and I loved to go to every wine country all over the planet.

My bucket list still had dozens of spots, and Machu Picchu and South America had been calling me for years. This was the trip of my dreams, and stepping out for a trip on my own felt amazing. I had done much solo travel over the years to wine country all over the world, but that was always for business. This trip was for me.

On the train ride back from Machu Picchu to Cusco, the tears streamed uncontrollably down my face. I had my "soul family" around me for support during my uncontrollable sobbing.

I didn't even know why I was crying. It started the moment I was reviewing my trip up Huayna Picchu. It came to me that the only challenge had been negotiating my heavy backpack.

It was only a day trip, so I didn't need to carry anything but water, food and a camera, but there I was trying to balance walking up, and down the very steep mountain with so much weight in my backpack, I might as well have been carrying bricks.

The reality of carrying too much crap with me suddenly hit. It was a perfect metaphor for my life. I was carrying around tons of emotional crap, and whatever that was, needed to be recognized and released.

At that moment, I knew that all of the emotional baggage I thought I successfully locked away, was only piled up inside of me, waiting to be dealt with. Shit.

Yes, a lot of shit.

Stupid stuff my from childhood, marriage, and god knows what else. All I could do was cry. Heart-wrenching sobs that overwhelmed and then calmed down. The minute I tried to speak again, they would return, and the cycle would repeat.

I then realized that I was having a complete and total meltdown.

Everyone in the group tried to console me with their own stories of mental breakdowns and misery to somehow help me manage my own.

I thought I had done much soul searching when I had pneumonia. I realised just how much more shit I was carrying around. I was just getting started.

The heavy backpack was the perfect metaphor for all the shit I was carrying: the perceived hurts, the loves lost, the unfulfilled dreams. OMG, what a crock of shit I was holding onto.

The memory of the two-hour train ride still makes me cry when I think about how silly I had been to hold onto all that shit for so long! What had that cost me?

I was 47 years old. I had accumulated 47 years of emotional baggage I could have dealt with and released years earlier.

The final two-hour bus ride from Ollantaytambo to Cusco with the gentle rocking of the bus through the mountains, allowed me to rest and think. What was I doing right here right now at this moment?

How was it that I came to join this particular soul family who spent so many hours helping me and sending healing vibrations? I was incredibly grateful for the opportunity, yet feeling so foolish that I showed such weakness by crying.

To this day, I may still break out in tears at a moment's notice. Rather than view that as weakness, I've stopped trying to hold back my emotions at any time.

I felt like I had been split wide open, which in itself was deeply healing. I was enjoying the freedom it provided. This feeling of freedom made it possible for me to join in on the ayahuasca session near the end of our journey.

I had been entirely against the thought of using the sacred ayahuasca, not because I've exclusively used alcohol as my drug of choice but because I heard that it often involved throwing up for hours. I couldn't imagine enjoying that part, no matter how mystical or spiritual the experience.

However, having cried my eyes out, I was now open and ready to try anything to experience the profound healing I needed.

"In the indigenous cultures of the Andes & Amazon are those who have allied with the plant teachers in allowing in ancient sacred ways, those who are ready and courageous to explore the inner dimensions of Truth. For in the revered ceremonies of what is termed 'Mother Ayahuasca' and to a lesser degree 'San Pedro', are inter-dimensional doorways that can, to the serious and prepared seeker, provide a life review, akin to what certain religions call the 'afterlife judgement, yet his occurs while the body and soul are yet united, in earthen life, and thus the soul is able to return and adjust. Ayahuasca is an incredible teacher, yet not for everyone, but for those who are ready to face the truth and work on self in a lens of amplified review. "
- James Tipton Tyberon

During the ceremony, as I felt the potion moving through my limbs, down my arms to the tips of my fingers, slithering like a snake through my veins, the colors began swirling through my brain with massive shots of light beaming through randomly.

It was like I was watching a movie about LSD from the '60s. There was a fantastic feeling of peace. Based on what I had heard, I had braced myself for a terrible experience with vomiting.

Yet there I was sitting quite still, knowing that my mind and my consciousness was experiencing something amazing. I nearly threw up the instant the foul tasting liquid poured by the Andean shaman entered my mouth. The expected vomiting did not occur, and at the moment, it felt like a nice buzz without any munchies.

It disgusted me to hear all the others in the room retching and screaming at random intervals, but I reminded myself that this was my experience, and it was my journey to take.

Tyb later told me that I hadn't swallowed enough and shouldn't have had any awareness or conscious thoughts while I was under the ayahuasca. I had indeed had an experience and was thrilled that I was able to excrete all the shit instead of throwing it up.

Sensations from this experience were noticeable in my body for months afterward.

The entire Machu Picchu experience was a massive transformation for me. Mentally, physically, emotionally, and spiritually my life was being reoriented. It was such a significant shift that it seemed from that point that almost everything in my life had shifted.

One of the most noticeable changes was that I agreed to start meditating again. Meditation had been a practice of mine on and off for the previous 25 years. I was never really sure why I stopped other than my life got "too busy."

One of my soul family, Sue, agreed to be my partner. We would communicate over Skype which meant I could enjoy my return to meditation practice with an experienced practitioner as my guide.

CHAPTER 6

Meditation Visions

Without warning, I saw the most beautiful, angelic butterfly-like creature, and I started to cry. Tears rolled down my face as I tried not to make any noise. This was my first meditation with Sue and, for some reason, I didn't want her to hear me crying.

The tears kept flowing as I saw this beautiful being, which was so amazing. The understanding that this beauty was Sue was like witnessing a miracle for me. More importantly, I saw a mirror image of myself.

I couldn't believe that I too was that beautiful. Growing up, I was used to being the tomboy; I never liked dressing up or worrying about makeup or fancy clothes. I never enjoyed dressing up for work.

It was such a shock and revelation to me, not just that such beauty could exist, but that I too, was that.

Sue told me that during a reading she had with Tyb, he said to her that she would meet another "aspect" of herself during the trip to Peru. We had connected on the trip, but not in a significant way.

While on the trip, there was no way I could have ever imagined such a profound and deep connection. I felt connected to my soul family, and Sue was part of that, but that initial connection was nothing like this.

It wasn't until I saw her as an aspect of myself in the meditation that I understood what she meant as she explained what Tyb had revealed.

I was incredulous, but the tears streaming down my face were recognition of the beauty that the universe had created – I was that beauty.

I knew from that moment on that, Sue and I were connected in a way that many people would associate with twin souls, but that's not the same as a different aspect of another human being.

It's as if we split off in different directions many thousands of years ago, but originated from the same life at some point. Crazy, I know. Utterly ridiculous is what I thought, but I couldn't deny the vision I had seen in the meditation.

Sue created the meditation as a simple way to help me get back into the practice of meditation, something I had done before and enjoyed. Somehow, I had let it slip entirely from my life.

So with my return to meditation, I gained more knowledge of my being from that one moment than I had amassed in my previous 47 years.

Intellectually, it seems crazy. However, deep in my heart, it makes complete sense. Everything shifted, and I knew what I had to do next.

Number one, I had to learn from her.

She had spent the last 55 years of her life meditating, searching, being a seeker of the higher spiritual realms, and I was much more of a pragmatist. I was an entrepreneur.

While I enjoyed the immense learning and understanding I was gaining from my practice of internal martial arts, Sue's knowledge and wisdom greatly exceeded anything I could have imagined for myself.

Sue took me on as a student, practicing meditation. She used Socratic questioning to keep challenging my beliefs and assumptions about what is, what the world looks like, and what possibilities lie beyond our immediate imagination.

There was an incredibly long reading list to help me catch up to speed. Books like: *The Emerald Tablets of Toth*, *The Book of Knowledge: The Keys of Enoch* and many others.

I began devouring books and information on the Internet, where people all over the planet were sharing their ideas.

It made the wine business look boring.

It made me challenge all the beliefs I had about what a "successful life" looked like.

It brought me to ask some fundamental questions:

Why was I here?

What did I come here to do?

What did I come here to BE?

I found an online community through my soul family from Peru. Many of us stayed in touch. Long before Facebook reached my generation, there were a whole series of forums where "light workers" and "earth keepers" could share their stories.

It was a complete disconnect from my life in suburban New Jersey. I didn't know how to reconcile this amazing universe I now saw and explored in my meditations with the physical world that made up my day to day living.

Through that one meditation, a daily practice of deeper and more profound meditation grew. I was at my little home in New Jersey, meditating, speaking, and connecting with Sue on the little island of Tasmania, Australia, all the way across the planet.

CHAPTER 7

Goodbye Milou

Milou was cowering in the bathroom, shaking violently. His eyes were going around in circles. It looked bad. My beautiful black Labrador seemed near death.

I screamed when I saw him and called for my son to come and help me get him out of the bathroom. This 75-pound animal had been such a mainstay in our lives. He was connected with nearly every beautiful memory we had.

He was quite big for our small house, but that made him all the more lovable. His boundless energy and bottomless hunger provided a spark for many tender and funny stories in our family.

I had noticed that his hips had been giving out on our daily walks, and he seemed to be in constant pain. Seeing him in terrible pain was too much.

I knew he needed immediate medical attention.

My daughter worked at a local veterinary office, and I immediately called her to see if we should bring the dog to where she was or if we should go to our regular vet.

She told us to bring him to her. The prognosis wasn't good. The veterinarian thought there was a chance he could be cured of the immediate balance and shaking problem, but there was nothing to do about his hips or loose bowels.

Painfully, we realized it was time to put Milou down.

Everyone who's had a pet they loved knows how heart-wrenching it is to lose a beloved companion. On top of all that normal sadness, I saw an added layer of symbology in my personal journey.

I began to notice a definite pattern of endings. My son, the last child at home, was finishing high school, and would be leaving for college in two months. My daughter was already out of the house and in college in Quebec.

The death of Milou was yet another massive ending of what had been so important in my life for so many years.

I jokingly said to a friend, "it's only a matter of time before I move to a mountain-top in China."

Little did I know.

I began seeing endings everywhere. It felt like everything I had previously lived and experienced needed to end so that something new could be created.

As it always does, time was marching onward. But somehow, now it felt like everything had a time limit. I began thinking about life in terms of the length of events: how long kids are in school, how long before they grew up and moved out, how long a dog lives.

We adopted Milou from a shelter. It was a battle with Jerome to agree to have a dog. The kids and I wore him down until he finally said yes. We were overjoyed.

We had stopped at a diner on our way to the shelter and picked the name first – Milou. We used to joke that he was the "anti - Milou" as the name Milou came from the dog in the French comic book Tin-Tin.

In that story, Milou was the small fluffy white dog who went on adventures with Tin-Tin. It was the perfect name.

When we told the shelter staff that we wanted to take the black Lab home, we got hit with bad news. They told us he couldn't go to a home with children. Oops. I didn't believe that a black Labrador could ever be anything but nice. The staff member said, "He had been abused, probably by children. He seems to react strangely around kids sometimes." That didn't dissuade us; we decided that Milou was coming home with us.

Sure enough, Milou was always strange; not around the kids, or me, but around every other stranger who came to the house. That turned out to be a good thing.

He became our trusty guard dog. This suited my purpose perfectly – I worked crazy hours, and as the kids got older, they were often home alone. His presence provided me with a certainty that no one was coming through the front door without permission.

Now, at that moment, he was gone. It was the end of an era.

In my mind, sweet Milou represented the last bit of my white-picket-fence dream. The kids, the husband, the house and the black Lab, once all present and accounted for, and now all fading.

That dream of a perfect little life had slipped away when Milou's life ended. Someone looking from the outside may have thought it silly, but I felt confident that it was time for something new.

CHAPTER 8

The Split

There it was, staring me in the face–formal separation after 24 years of marriage.

I couldn't believe Jerome wanted to move out of the house. I was the one asking for a separation, and he wanted to move out. Jerome didn't want a separation, but if we were going to separate, he wanted to move.

"That is crazy!" I thought.

Although in some ways, it made perfect sense. He had a very long commute on the bus from New Jersey into Manhattan every day, and his move would allow that to be easier and shorter.

The financial realities of this decision began to hit me. My wine business was growing, but travel and expenses ate up a huge portion of the profits.

I had lost almost all of my 401K money to terrible real estate deals after the market crash of 2008, and my stock portfolio had lost 80% of its value from its high a few years earlier.

I was suddenly afraid of what it would be like to live on my own. There were important questions such as: "how could I keep up the mortgage payments?" and, "how could we get freed up from underwater real estate deals that were using up all our cash?"

We had created a very comfortable life. If I hadn't invested heavily in bad real estate deals, we would have been sitting pretty. That mistake was hurting badly at this point.

There were no easy answers. As it was, the numbers were incredibly tight for me to live on my own as my husband tried to find accommodation in Manhattan.

Even with an excellent salary, it was going to be hard. Apartment rent in Manhattan was through the roof.

I couldn't even remember why we argued so much, just that it was constant. I'm not sure what changed so dramatically.

We had been very much in sync and very much in love when it all started. The kids came quickly, and our wish list of things we wanted to do seemed to have many things checked off.

We had rafted down the Grand Canyon and raised two beautiful children. We often traveled to exotic places. We had successful careers. We accomplished many of the things we wanted.

Even though I had made some horrible real estate decisions, we were still in good shape financially with one household. With two, it was going to be a challenge.

Trying to meet the mortgage payments for bad loans on Las Vegas investments began to jeopardize the money we needed to pay for my son's college education. My stress levels were constantly rising.

I wasn't about to let that happen, so we stopped the mortgage payments where we were underwater. We tried to negotiate with the banks for better terms and a short sale. What a nightmare.

None of the programs President Obama had put in place to help people in financial trouble after the real estate crash could help. That help was only for owner-occupied homes and not for rental units.

The real estate market in Las Vegas for new construction had collapsed, and I was financially screwed. The stress strained our marriage past the breaking point.

We had a good marriage for many years. Then it seemed to turn into a mediocre relationship with most of our attention focused on the kids. The kids were amazing – intelligent, caring, and friendly. They were also the entire focus of our life. When they left home to go to college, and our dog died, somehow it felt like I had "done" the family thing and I needed a change.

I had retired from my job and started my own growing business. I could see how the circles of life step in. I needed to act and not hesitate. I didn't want to wait until it was time to retire again to start living my life.

With all this change and inner turmoil, it began to feel like I was just going through the motions of being the "happy wife." Some call this a mid-life crisis. Maybe it was, but something had to change.

I didn't know exactly what it was going to look like, but I was ready for something new. I needed to get out of the old pattern even if it meant getting out of my marriage after 24 years.

I knew what a cliché that is among empty nesters. I never thought that I was only staying in the marriage "because of the kids," but once they were gone, my life felt empty. I was caught up in my own melodrama.

My mind was firm that I wanted a separation, but when the time came, and Jerome actually moved out, all the fear and insecurity moved in.

I was frozen. I had always been very decisive, and now I couldn't decide anything. Fear was crowding me everywhere:

> Fear of being alone.
> Fear of loss.
> Fear of moving.
> Fear of not being able to support myself.

Everything I was doing stemmed from a place of insecurity. I was terrified; afraid I was doing this all wrong.

CHAPTER 9

Hurricane Sandy

The first time I realised my central gas heating wasn't working was on Election Day, November 2012. I woke up seeing my breath making mist. OMG, I was freezing! What happened to my fire? What happened to the heater?

The electricity had been out for exactly one week following Hurricane Sandy. The prognosis for the electricity returning anytime soon was not good. The massive storm had wreaked major havoc across the states of New York and New Jersey.

In the days after the storm, my friends and neighbors began "roughing it." We started practicing off-grid living and the sharing economy. You never fully realise how much you depend on everything until it's gone.

Keeping my fireplace going for partial heating of the house, using candles to see during the long nights and sharing my neighbors' generator with a massively long electrical cord through our backyards were some of the practical accommodations we made.

These efforts allowed for some relative comfort, including charging my phone and some Internet access. Thank goodness, not all the cell towers were down. However, this morning I had a new problem.

What the hell had happened to the heat? I saw that the fire had gone out in the fireplace, but I couldn't understand why my gas heater hadn't turned on. I was completely bewildered.

It was Election Day, the first Tuesday in November. My immediate agenda was to throw on some sweat pants, head down to the fire station to vote and grab some of the coffee the police and fire squad had been graciously providing since the whole town was stranded in place.

There was already a line to vote, and I began chatting to the woman beside me. She didn't have a fireplace. She had been getting so cold she had resorted to boiling water on her gas-fired kitchen stove to heat the kitchen.

She explained that even though her heater was gas, it wouldn't work without the electronic ignition. I was furious. Why would they make devices that couldn't be lit with a match? It was ridiculous.

However, at least that explained the heater. I went back to burning every scrap of wood from the backyard to keep the house warm. Keeping the house warm was a big deal since I couldn't go anywhere.

The gas stations couldn't pump gas without electricity. Because of the damage and the cleanup, we were all advised to stay off the roads unless it was critical.

I was back to "off the grid" living. I was grateful that despite the hardships, we were enjoying great camaraderie on our street. All our neighbors were providing fantastic support to each other.

That was a welcome contrast with the stark reality of the aftermath of the storm. We were all in this together, and we shared whatever was necessary.

I was busy testing out a tiny solar device to power my phone and trying to make a passive heating system I saw on the Internet using aluminum cans and some black spray paint. The design was completely messed up, but it kept me busy.

I spent a lot of time gathering and sawing wood from around the neighborhood. I was grateful for my new Stihl chainsaw. My brothers called it the "light, girly model." Whatever, I was having fun.

It was like camping out while still having a bed and lots of warm comforters. In my case, I also had a giant wine cellar in the basement. Not bad for roughing it in the woods.

The real issue for me had nothing to do with the minor inconvenience of keeping life going at home. Staying warm was an easy problem to solve, as there was firewood to scavenge and burn, and somehow, I managed to keep my phone charged and operating. The most severe consequences had to do with my business.

The storm had begun innocently enough, the wind and rain battering the house were not unusual. Things started to get interesting when the lights went out. It was dusk, and I was hoping it wouldn't be a prolonged outage.

I stepped outside to see what was going on. I heard and saw blue lights pop as the streetlights blew. With the lights all gone, the street was immediately blanketed in darkness.

In my many years in New Jersey, I had seen many storms. Most were not a big deal, but this one had been in the news as it headed up the Atlantic coast. We had plenty of time to prepare, and I felt ready for anything.

I had learned how to drag as many things into the basement as possible from outside to avoid the danger of flying objects. I gathered lots of dry wood for my new fireplace insert that heated the whole house.

In the years that passed since meeting my soul family in Machu Picchu, and developing a close relationship with Sue, I had often traveled Down Under to her Vortex Healing Centre.

Spending time in Tasmania in a completely off-the-grid house taught me some things about being prepared.

I had a large 20-gallon tank of water in the basement. I had dried food in the pantry. I had candles, canned food, flashlights, and batteries. I was ready and not frightened at all.

It was normal for the electricity to flicker in my old house because I was out at the end of the grid. I was all set to get back to reading a good book and relaxing through the storm with or without electricity.

I loaded up the fire and settled in for the night.

The next morning the bad news hit me in the face. The old reliable landline was still working, and the ringing snapped me back to reality.

"Did you hear what happened to Fedway?" the voice asked. My stomach sank. "No, what?" When I worked at the Fedway warehouse, sandbags were always on hand because the buildings in Kearny were a high flood risk.

However, the owner knew all that, so I was sure that they had taken necessary precautions and were well protected during this storm.

"I can't believe you didn't hear," the voice went on. "Fedway lost their inventory in every one of their warehouses due to the flooding."

My mind reeled at the scope of this awful news. This could trash my business. I barely heard the voice continue, "But Richard is going to get it back, hopefully before Thanksgiving."

While I knew that Richard was a fantastic man and that if anyone could make such an amazing thing happen it was him, I was deeply concerned that my business cash flow would dry up to nothing in the meantime.

I got the full scoop later. It turned out that a freak tidal wave in the ocean ran UP the Kearny River and flooded the warehouses, causing this catastrophe. Interestingly, only Fedway's warehouses had been ruined.

The damage totaled over $125 million. The scope of the devastation meant that it made the national news, not just the local news. The pictures of the carnage seemed surreal.

The company had stocked up on inventory as the period from Thanksgiving to Christmas is the peak liquor and wine season. Cardboard boxes with their entire inventory were stacked up 20 feet high in some parts of the warehouse.

The flooding was only six feet deep in the main warehouse, but soggy cardboard boxes couldn't hold the weight on top, and everything came crashing down, one box on top of another in a horrendous domino effect.

Richard was able to move mountains. He got the warehouses cleaned up, sterilized and ready to move. He found 50 trucks to move supply, and he rallied all of his suppliers, employees, and the community the instant he saw what had happened.

Most people I know would have walked away. It seemed like such an impossible task. Even with his entire inventory gone, all the delivery trucks ruined and the warehouses damaged, Richard endured.

It was a remarkable testament to not only his business skills and amazing willpower, but mostly, to the reputation he had built with everyone over the past decades. That made everyone WANT to help him as much as possible.

Watching Fedway rebuild itself over the next few weeks was like watching a Phoenix rising, uplifting, and emotional for us all. I felt utterly helpless because all this magic was not going to make a difference for my situation.

The company was able to get the warehouses cleaned out and sanitized with a professional disaster relief team that worked around the clock. All of the mechanics of the conveyor system were redone and tested. The new inventory came from across the country and across the world to replace what was lost.

With such a limited time frame, Richard decided to focus on resupplying only the top few hundred inventory SKU numbers. Smaller brands, which included all my fine wines, would have to wait until January.

My business was screwed, and I was afraid.

Very afraid.

CHAPTER 10

Time To Move

I stood there, horrified as thoughts of fear overwhelmed me.

I had done it again. I had worked myself into a frenzy as a certified workaholic, even in my so-called retirement.

My wine marketing consulting company was supposed to be a part-time job, a kind of "hobby," but with the full-time benefit of staying in the wine business.

Traveling around the world, drinking great wine and eating great food had never been a drawback. Here I was again, working crazy hours and panicked out of my mind with the disaster that was going to wipe me out. Quickly, I realised that this was not what I wanted.

How did I get here again? There was no one to blame, no boss, no excuses, just the face in the mirror.

What was driving me to act in the opposite way of how I wanted to?

I'd felt so driven to succeed, to be important, to sell more, to do more. I had been trying to prove something to somebody, somewhere. The absurdity of it all weighed heavily on my heart.

I had created all of this. I had become a big success once again, but I still felt unhappy. I knew deep inside that there was something more. I was supposed to be doing something more than living a carefree life of eating and drinking.

Everything came to a grinding halt for a full week after Hurricane Sandy. Being without power and heat was one thing, but the lack of inventory to sell was the final nail in the coffin.

My two busiest months, November and December, and even into January of the next year, were going to be a big fat goose egg. This thought pushed me over the top.

I felt frustration at the prospect of not being busy. I had trained myself to work so much that I didn't even know how to think about not being busy during the typically manic holiday season.

I was feeling a fear of quiet time. Yet, I wasn't willing to create being busy to make these disturbing thoughts disappear. I had to rethink my life – again.

I began to face the fact that I wanted more! It wasn't about the money, prestige, or recognition. I wanted to feel like I was doing something important for my inner self—for my spiritual self.

I was already traveling to Tasmania, Australia to visit the Vortex Healing Centre along Elephant Pass a few times a year, but up to now, that was just something I did to dabble in stillness.

In my contemplation, I realized that I longed to be there in the incredible stillness of nature—watching stars, watching plants grow, watching birds and crazy animals. I was ready to drop everything and go.

The realities of such a decision started floating through my consciousness. I had only one sales rep working for me, and he was as stunned by the storm as I had been.

When I asked him to continue hitting the pavement with the brands I had in Manhattan, which had returned to normal a few weeks after the storm, he chose to work on his more lucrative website business instead.

I couldn't blame him. His other gig was creating more cash and Christmas was around the corner. I felt abandoned and utterly alone. I took a breath and decided to change everything once again.

A confirmation showed up in the form of a former colleague who had worked with my brands in the past. He was looking for a new job.

My old job was going to be his new job. We immediately started getting him set up to replace me and take over my company. The stars aligned. I got ready to retire. Again.

This time, I was going to be sure. I decided I would make the jump to live in Tasmania. My permanent retirement!

In the past, a running joke was that someday I was going to leave everything behind and live on a mountaintop in China. I had no idea how close to the truth those words would turn out to be.

My mountaintop turned out to be a beautiful picturesque hill along Elephant Pass, Tasmania an island state in Australia. I was ready to leave it all behind.

Almost. As the move got underway, all the objects stayed behind, but I brought an unplanned stowaway, a giant suitcase full of my guilt.

Somehow, I couldn't leave that behind, yet. I guess I wasn't ready to acknowledge that it was OK for me to be happy and choose a completely different lifestyle.

Extra baggage or not, I decided to start a whole new life at 52. I was determined to finally and truly awaken.

CHAPTER 11

Sell The House

The main obstacle to the big move was deciding what to do with my house. In my old thinking, I had always pictured that beautiful place as our family home forever. A place for the kids to come home to and one day bring their kids.

I wasn't nearly ready to leave the memories behind. There were so many wonderful memories of watching our family grow up in our beautiful New Jersey home—complete with rickety stairs, a dungeon-like basement, and a beautiful backyard. It even boasted a permaculture food forest in the front.

Memories push their way forward. Memories like walking my daughter to kindergarten a block away, just a few weeks after moving in. Here I had watched the ebb and flow of life as they grew older, matured and finally moved out.

Most of my friends lived in the neighborhood. Feelings and memories of deep friendships wrapped around me like a warm, comfortable blanket in the wintertime.

I knew I wanted to go to Tasmania, but I don't think I was ready to leave. I was not as prepared to let it all go as I had thought.

All the energy I felt as I clung to those memories made it hard for the house to sell.

I was holding on tightly to the emotions and memories of what had been my home for over 22 years. Even though I had traveled often, this place had been my base so long it felt impossible to let it go.

I felt guilty taking the house away from my kids as if it were a security blanket for them. As it turns out, the security blanket was only in my mind. Panic arose when I thought about trying to make a new home 11,000 km away in someplace where people spoke with a funny accent.

Even though I was spending a month at a time in Australia regularly, this house was still my refuge. It was someplace I could call my own. MY home.

I started by selling some things on Craigslist and eBay, but it quickly became evident I was a closet hoarder.

My kids and now ex-husband had begged me to have garage sales over the years, but I had always refused. I was positive that I might need that stuff someday.

I always thought that some things just needed fixing, and then they would be "good as new." I still had stuff, nearly untouched, that we had brought over in a container from France 22 years earlier. It was all just stuff.

Stuff full of memories. Stuff that reminded me of the kids. All the things I was "going to do someday." Everything held meaning for me.

I'm sure that's how all hoarders think. We need our stuff. I was instantly reminded of the "stuff" I had carried around in my backpack while climbing Machu Picchu. That stuff had led to my meltdown on the train ride after the climb. I was still obsessed with stuff.

I was so devastated trying to pack up all my stuff, that I couldn't finish packing. I had to get my sister-in-law and brother to help me sort out all the useless crap. They graciously helped, and we eventually filled a few boxes to send to Tasmania.

After many more tears, I was just plain stuck.

I couldn't pick up a single object without crying. I had chosen the divorce. I had chosen to move. I had chosen a new life, and I was still stuck, sorting through objects I believed had so much meaning.

Even though I knew only the memories mattered, and that I would carry them with me forever, I was paralyzed and couldn't be consoled. I felt incapable of making even the smallest decision about the house. I finally gave up and allowed them to help me finalize the process.

They did all the heavy lifting. They coordinated the dumpsters and supervised the installation of the new kitchen appliances.

The carnage was amazing. There were two giant dumpsters filled with garbage and many weekends of garage sales. I gave away objects by the carload–one price all you can carry. After that, the Salvation Army carted off the rest in several carloads.

There is a saying: "lead, follow or get out of the way." I was just in the way. I kept picking up objects and crying, getting nothing done.

As my flight to Tasmania approached, emotionally all I could manage to do was get my suitcases and myself to the airport on time.

On top of that, I carried a fresh batch of guilt because I left a giant pile of stuff for my sister-in-law and brother to deal with. They even did the prep work to ready the house for sale. I was grateful that they came to my rescue.

I still wasn't clear. I remained conflicted, clinging to my house full of memories. I felt like such a failure. I had set off to live my new life, and part of me was still stuck in the past.

Even though the physical preparations were complete, I still had a lot of "letting go" and personal healing to do before I could finally bring myself to sell the house.

"Yes, the Internet is that bad here where we live."

"Access to the world is better on "Monkey Island" then here along Elephant Pass."

– Barbara Longué

PART II

My Tassie Life

CHAPTER 12

Life Down Under

Physically moving from one side of the world to the other is a daunting and courageous undertaking. By making such a decision, I mistakenly assumed I was home free, or at least close.

Through the months and years that followed, I had lots of new things to get used to. There was the strange accent, different foods, laid-back lifestyle, and a hundred other things.

However, nothing was anywhere near as difficult as the emotional upheaval that seemed to accompany every new thing. Somehow, despite the appeal and excitement, almost everything hooked into some memory of the past.

I had some feeling that I had failed, or had chosen poorly, in taking such a bold move in declaring my independence.

While life has regular ups and downs, in New Jersey or Tasmania, I seemed to magnify everything through the lens of the emotional tsunami I had unleashed with my life-changing decision.

CHAPTER 13

Tassie Dreams

Tasmania, or Tassie, as Australians call it, is an island about the size of Vermont and New Hampshire put together, but with only one-quarter of the population.

The vistas are breathtaking. The mountains stand strong. Ancient hardwood forests stand as they have for thousands of years. Stunningly beautiful white sand beaches complete the landscape.

Add to this a unique collection of wild animals, beautiful flowers and unusual birds, some of which are found nowhere else in the world, topping it all off with a cool climate. Those of you who have been to Australia and sweated your way through the visit know just what I mean.

I was experiencing the most radical change imaginable. I left New Jersey, the most densely populated state in America, to live on an island that time seemed to have forgotten.

The stereotypical picture Americans have of kangaroos hopping through the streets of Australia isn't accurate in the cities, but they show up in spades in the sparsely populated towns of Tassie.

Here, it's every man for himself. The Wallabies, pademelons, wombats, echidnas and many other hopping creatures you've never heard of emerge at dusk, drawn to the roadsides as they begin their nocturnal walkabouts.

> Question: Why did the pademelon cross the road?
> Answer: To get to the other side.

Don't groan. Here that punchline, to the very old joke, is completely accurate. All wildlife has somewhere to go. They wake up at dusk and find that the paths they instinctively follow, continue on the other side of the road.

Driving home from our neighboring small village of St. Marys one evening, it looked just like a cartoon. Heads were popping up out of the field as the car drove by. They were all looking around. Thinking. You could almost see the thought bubbles above their heads, saying, "Time to cross the road!"

As the car kept moving forward up the hill, they all began hopping towards the road as if drawn by a magnet, utterly oblivious that a 4000-pound car was hurtling toward them as they started to cross.

Occasionally one would look over at the car, then look at the road and keep hopping on a direct collision course with the heavy steel bumper.

Thankfully we avoided all collisions that day. However, from then on, I avoided driving after dusk. The number of semi-flat animals on the road is a silent witness to how many of these rare and beautiful animals endure a terrible and painful death.

Now for the house. Sue purchased an old cow paddock of several acres some 22 years earlier. She built her own modest off-grid, sustainable house long before it became fashionable to do so.

Three-quarters of the estate was fenced off to preserve native forests, and on the remaining section, she built the house. She completed her landscaping with a beautiful array of native Australian and Tasmanian plants.

The property boasts a picturesque view of the sea right from the house. A heavenly show that would make stargazers envious is visible every night from the upstairs bedroom through the large sliding glass door.

I had often heard Sue talk about the incredible energy on the property. She had been working to protect and develop this unique vortex of powerful energy flow.

The spot where the energy exits in the earth are amazing. More than 90% of visitors feel something when they stand on "the vortex." Even though most don't know what it is or how it works, that doesn't change the tingling they get in their hands or feet when they stand near this sacred and powerful place.

I had previously visited only a few sacred sites around the planet before I visited this vortex. My first experience was remarkable. Almost overnight, my sensitivity to all my intuition increased.

The entire place felt like a fantastic field of pure and unlimited potentiality. Anything could happen there. I could almost see quantum shifts happening in myself and others right before my eyes.

I did some research into quantum physics to help me understand more about vibration in matter and energy. I was amazed at how particles can come into and out of existence. I didn't understand much of it, but I could feel what they were describing there in that place.

We were anxious to create a place where Sue could continue her massage therapy and naturopathy practice.

Also, we wanted to create a space for deep healing and spiritual transformation. In its pure and native state, the land already radiated healing and transformative energy. All we needed to do was get people to understand what was available and come for a visit.

We were excited to find a local tradesperson who had just started making yurts. Note to self: never buy an artisan beta model without a guarantee he will fix it until it's right.

Yep. We were the guinea pigs for his new design. We wanted something functional that would blend with the environment. Not a permanent building, but something that would allow for an extended stay on the property.

His design of a circular canvas structure turned out to be a big tent. After a few missteps, everything worked. We now had this beautiful big yurt for lodging constructed a little way from the house. The Vortex Healing Center was born.

St. Marys is our nearest town, located 20 km inland from the shore along the Fingal Valley plateau. It's a quaint old mining town with small houses and a few shops.

It reminded me of something out of the *Andy Griffith Show* back when everyone knew everyone else in town, and they chatted regularly. Easy when there are only 600 people.

Andy's aunt Bea always claimed that there was no problem "a good sit down, and some apple pie can't fix." That's the way the town feels. It's a throwback to a much gentler time.

The town has many modern services: a hospital, school, pub, hotel, and even an organic grocery store. What else could you want? A movie theatre? Not within 100 miles, but who cares?

I believed I was ready to set out on my newest adventure. My goal was to have a healing center where we could follow a sustainable lifestyle living off the grid.

I was going to grow lots of my own food, connect with people around the world through modern technology via videoconference, and maintain my new coaching business. I was going to live my dream lifestyle.

CHAPTER 14

Losing My Identity

Ouch. I was struggling. Sometimes the dreams we hold don't include all the details of reality as it might unfold. That's probably good because if we knew about the struggles, we might not ever take the adventure.

Sue had purchased a small retail shop to improve her cash flow in the town of St. Marys. It was a combined retail gift shop and post office. Owning the business allowed her to start the visa process to allow me to work and stay in Australia.

The sudden shock of moving from my high-intensity work and lifestyle to one of slow contemplation freaked me out. I found myself sorely missing my old life.

My visa wasn't going to be ready for a few months, and I wasn't allowed to work until it was finalized. With not enough to do, I went back to the States to finish the transition of my wine marketing business.

The reality of this transition was slowly sinking in. Living in France for seven years and studying enology in Burgundy and Bordeaux, the wine business had been in my blood for all of my adult life.

Wine was my first love in France. Being in France provided all kinds of other benefits. In my second year there, I met the Frenchman who would become my husband.

Thirty-five years later, I realized that my entire adult life was encapsulated in the wine business. Even on vacation, most years included at least one visit to a winery, or visiting and sharing meals with my winemaker friends, eating great food and drinking great wine.

On top of that, I was a workaholic. My entire identity was tied to my work. With the tiny emotional space left, I was a wife and a mother. There was one thing that seemed to get lost in all that, which was ME. I was struggling to get out of the old and into the new, and it was becoming obvious I was in for a journey.

A year or so after my move to Tasmania, during a trip back to the States; I met up with some very dear friends in the wine business, Randy & Lucy. As usual, the visit included sharing a great meal and tasty wine at a favorite restaurant in New Jersey.

The waiter didn't have half of the food we wanted to order, and there was an extended delay in the meal coming out. My old self would have become annoyed at the situation because I was always in a hurry to get to the next appointment – always rushing into the future.

This time was different. I felt relaxed and enjoyed the time describing how the meditation center was coming along. Halfway through the meal, Lucy asked, "Who ARE you? And what did you do with my friend?"

We had a good laugh. I felt happy that my newly found calm and ability to stay in the present moment was improving. I could now stay present and focused in a normal situation for longer than a short meditation or yoga class.

I genuinely enjoyed being able to spend time with my wine friends.

While with my friends, it was easy to describe how I had radically transformed my life in an entirely new way. Back home, in Tasmania, what I couldn't do well was feeling at peace with all that "extra time."

I was still missing the excitement, travel, and all the fun of wine tastings and the associated hoopla. I was struggling with knowing who I was. If I wasn't Ms. Wine Expert, then what should I DO and what should I BE?

Part of me wanted to do nothing and meditate on the top of a mountain all day, and part of me wanted to shake up the sleepy little town and make big things happen. I didn't know what things, just BIG things.

Something felt to me like I might be drinking too much. Some part of me wanted to justify excessive wine consumption because I HAD worked in the business previously. As if that were an excuse to overindulge.

Most importantly, I wondered if I could, indeed make a difference. I wondered if I was still important.

In my previous business, I was lucky that I had started at the very bottom rung and worked my way up through the multitude of "business ladders" to reach the pinnacle at Fedway.

In that process, you learn to tell who is sucking up because they thought I was important and who was a friend. Because of the shift brought on by my first retirement, I didn't have any delusions about how people would react to me when I was no longer in a position of great buying power.

Strength by loyalty is a chant my coach JT Foxx uses all the time, and it was apparent after my "first" retirement how important loyalty is. Some key clients vanished overnight, and other clients like Gary Vaynerchuk or Randy Burke went out of their way to allow me to bring them deals. I am forever grateful that they believed in me through thick and thin. Moreover, I still smile whenever I see them and know that this is a crucial sign of their ethics and integrity in a hectic world.

My second retirement was much more challenging. Not only did I not have the big buying power I had enjoyed at Fedway, but I also wasn't even in the boutique business anymore. No one in Tasmania knew me for my business acumen.

I was entirely different for them as a business consultant, a coach, a healer, and a meditator. I came in as a blank slate. I was starting once again at the bottom, and I had to show people who I truly was.

It didn't help that I was still asking that question myself.

CHAPTER 15

Leaving Family Behind

I was moving to Australia, 10,000 miles away from what had been my home for decades. The one overwhelming fear was leaving my family behind.

The children had gone off to college. I remembered how challenging the transition to college had been for me. Growing up and leaving home is a normal milestone for every kid, but I knew how long it took me to make that transition.

I was uncertain about the consequences of moving halfway across the planet. And not just halfway across the planet, but to a tiny island where services were sometimes intermittent.

I was also concerned about leaving my mother. My father had died a few years earlier after a difficult bout with Alzheimer's and related complications. I knew that she still needed a lot of support to be settled and feel calm.

Every time I thought of my children, I realised that I was still calling them my kids as if they were still three years old.

I knew they were no longer three years old. On the contrary, they're amazing young adults, but I still wondered, "When do you stop calling them your kids?"

The answer, of course, is never. They will always be my children, and part of me still sees the adorable little three-year-olds they used to be. I remember with great fondness the family unity that created and supported those children and the life they had.

So now it gets a little weird. One of the things that delayed completing my move to Tasmania was that, even though mentally I had already decided what I wanted, some part of me was waiting to make sure that's what I really and truly wanted to do.

I know that sounds crazy.

When I dropped everything and moved to France after graduating from Georgetown University, it wasn't a big deal because I had nothing to lose and no heavy attachments.

I didn't own a car. There was no money in the bank. All I needed to do was get enough money to buy a plane ticket and go over there.

Now, I had a business, a career, and a family – a family that was split up, and all the kids grown. It still felt like I had a lot to lose. I patiently waited to make sure that this was what I wanted to do.

I knew that my daughter, Camille, was settled and committed to becoming a veterinarian. My son Mike seemed to be settled on a good path as well.

I knew both intellectually and emotionally that, whether it was a midlife crisis or some other influence, I had to create the next chapter of my life. Most importantly, that meant choosing myself first.

That choice was the primary reason for the divorce, and ultimately choosing to move to Tasmania.

I felt incredibly guilty even though I knew the kids were grown, had graduated and begun lives of their own. They were real contributing adults now, not just big kids in college.

I felt even more guilty about leaving my mom. That caused an enormous amount of anxiety. Some of that still lingers at the time of this writing as her dementia has worsened and come to a head.

The wisdom I was then missing was the truth about creating a relationship. I held deep connections and would keep in meaningful contact with both children and my mom, no matter what the distance. Starting that practice has lowered the volume of the guilt microphone.

My technique has been to call, write, email, or text them every day, even if it's a tiny thing. Even if I miss a day, I still think of them and ask them to connect to that.

Initially, I would forward emails that I thought were relevant to my kids. My son gave me a powerful piece of wisdom when he said, "I want to know what you're thinking and what you are doing. I don't care about something else you've read."

I was shocked. I thought I was useful, but that wasn't how the children wanted to connect – one more beautiful lesson.

Instead, I began taking a photo chronology of my life in Tasmania and where my travels were taking me. Using the pictures as the mainstay, I added a few words about what was happening to me to engage their imagination and emotion.

It was a wonderful surprise when they started emailing back spontaneously. My daughter began sending photos of her walk across London Park. It felt like I could see through their eyes what was of interest to them. It has become a beautiful tradition that I continue to this day.

My mom's condition has made it more and more challenging to operate a computer. So now I text a photo to her, and she can see and enjoy that. It also provides a great starting point for our next phone conversation.

We communicate by phone daily, even though she doesn't remember my calls or remember much at all about recent events. Her memories and all recollections are quite colorful.

The one side-benefit to my workaholic tendencies had been my optimistic retirement expectations. I had once intended to retire at 40, but then my own business took over and delayed that a few years.

Even with all of that, I was blessed to be able to create this new retirement in Tasmania. I felt gratitude that I was young enough to be able to enjoy the opportunity to start a completely new life, doing something different, and transforming myself yet again.

CHAPTER 16

I Get Paid For That Now

"I get paid for that now," was my response. It was as simple as that. The question had been, "Can I meet with you and pick your brain? Can you swing by my office?" or "Can we meet for breakfast, lunch, or dinner, or drinks?"

It seemed that everyone wanted to pick my brain. This was the third call in a week, and the third person to get the response, "Yeah, sure, but I get paid for that now."

I love helping people with their business, with their problems, whatever that may be. It turned out I was usually pretty good at solving questions about business growth, employees, or just about anything related to the wine business, retail operations, and restaurants.

So, my knowledge and ability to act and think quickly was regularly solicited. As much as I enjoyed the interaction of sharing what I knew with friends and acquaintances from the industry, I realised what a time suck it had become.

At the same time, I knew people were getting paid big money to coach business owners on different aspects of a business. These included how to grow a business quickly, or how to get a life, or how to eliminate stress in the workplace.

Like most people involved in personal development and business, I had been active online in many communities. One high-profile coach had been sending me emails that made me think, "Oh, I can do that."

I made an appointment to meet with my colleague and friend who needed help. I explained what I explain to most business owners who think the problem is the economy or the way the world works, or their competitors.

In almost every case, it comes down to a few simple things that show up over and over again. Sometimes the business owner is a control freak and can't delegate. Sometimes the owner isn't considering creative solutions that might come from going in a new direction. Sometimes the owner won't take enough risk because there are no guarantees.

The truth is that the problems always originate with the business owner and not the environment.

That first client gave me the validation that I had vast knowledge and good communication techniques. My ideas were strong, and all I needed was a way to get in front of those people who wanted an effective transformation process.

I knew that I could help a lot of business owners and others who wanted significant change in their life or business. If their life *was* their business, like me, I knew I could help them get their life back.

I hired a coach for myself and joined a mastermind. The best part for me was in knowing there was someone I could share my most personal fears with.

They were on my team and wanted my success. They could help me walk through all the parts that I was avoiding and not facing.

Being in a mastermind is still something I really enjoy. It's great to have people all around the world that you feel close to because we have the same goal of transforming lives in a significant way.

We've maintained the same mastermind group, made up of people who can support each other at any time of the day or night. There is always someone awake in the zone that we're in.

My biggest challenge became a practical one. We take broadband with unlimited access for granted in the United States and Europe. I guess that's true everywhere, except not in the place I chose to be, the small island of Tasmania.

My online coaching business was my link back to the "big world." I could feel like I was still connected to some part of the old me that ran big businesses, had started my own business and ran an $18 million division for an even bigger business.

As you might suspect, things were about to change.

CHAPTER 17

Internet Addiction

I wouldn't have described myself as an addict. I had no clue how addicted I was using Siri and Google 24/7. Any time I had a question in my mind, or wanted to send off an email, binge-watch 18 hours of Netflix or anything else, it had been instantly available for so much, and for so many hours, of my life.

It began to dawn on me that somewhere inside I thought of Google and Siri as my constant companions. I had to start "unlearning" being so dependent on these modern conveniences.

Even now, in this remote area of Australia, unlimited Internet is not available. On top of the limited availability, the broadband we have access to is incredibly expensive compared to the rates in my old life, or seemingly anywhere else in the world.

MONEY, FAMILY, SEX & HAPPINESS

When I first arrived at Sue's place, the only way she had a telephone connection was through an enormous antenna on the roof that connected to a wire that literally plugged into her phone.

It felt like a bad nightmare from some apocalyptic movie about a devastating future. I wasn't able to make any phone calls or connect to the Internet while at her place.

I immediately began an enormous research project finding topographical maps to see how I could create a connection to the rest of the world.

I found a company in Brisbane that did that geo-mapping. This enabled us to get a new type of repeater in the house that would connect to the giant antenna on the roof.

That meant we could use the telephone signal as long as we were using any Telstra phone plan. It also allowed me to buy broadband using a Telstra Wi-Fi modem.

Then, the heavens parted just a few months after my arrival as NBN Australia announced an upgrade plan. They had been working on a stronger network to increase Internet access across the country, especially in remote zones.

Their goal was to bring the entire country up to a standard platform and propel it forward. They announced that the satellite connection at Sue's place was being upgraded and an entirely new satellite would be launched within six months.

I was ecstatic, although I didn't think I could last six months. The thought of not being able to connect easily to my family via email was so dramatic it sent me to tears at the mere whisper of it.

The six months passed. With what I now know, this is the normal pace of progress here. The new announcement put the date out an additional year. The reality was that the saga lasted for three years.

Even though the new satellite had launched, and the upgrades installed, unlimited internet access is still unavailable. The Internet remains slow and occasionally will turn off for no obvious reason.

On good days, I can do all of my live connections via Zoom or Skype, or any one of the numerous ways we connect online. Most days aren't good days. It's funny how much we take for granted.

In case you think I'm exaggerating, here is a funny story to make my point.

Sue and I went on a vacation with her whole family to an island in Thailand. Sue's sister had passed away, and the family got together to honor her life and support each other in that emotional time.

Her sister lived alone and had become sick with pneumonia; she died quite unexpectedly without telling anyone how sick she was.

In her will, she had made provisions for the entire family to take a trip. The family decided to go to Thailand because her sister had loved that country and had travelled there often.

Sue's sister-in-law, Robyn, made arrangements and found a great resort on a beautiful island. I called it Monkey Island because of the national park dedicated to monkeys located there.

On "Monkey Island" I had great, unlimited Internet that was stable and free. For a short time, I had the joy of getting my work done without having to sign on and sign off 12 times.

Because I have adapted and learned many amazing techniques to get so much done in so little time, while I was on vacation, I could create a full-time income working only an hour or two a day.

Yes, the Internet is that bad here where we live. Access to the world is better on "Monkey Island" then here along Elephant Pass. Oh, the joys of living in the middle of the forest overlooking the ocean.

That limitation is still a challenge for me. Someday it may change, but for now, I keep my fingers crossed and hold my breath that the Internet flows on the day I need it.

That makes me wonder: "Do I still have an addiction if I don't have access to the substance of my desire?"

CHAPTER 18

Am I Living In A Cave?

Damn it. It was raining again, and I had to step outside the house, walk through the rain to go to the bathroom. The bathroom, or toilet room, is in a separate building from the main house and is on a septic tank.

It made me crazy to have to walk outside in the rain, in the wind, at night or whenever, to go to the bathroom. I couldn't understand how someone would build a house with an expensive septic tank and not integrate it indoors.

None of that felt like a problem unless it was dark outside or raining, especially if it was cold, dark and raining. I felt like such a wimp, but I couldn't get used to the level of asceticism I had agreed to when I moved to the house in the middle of the forest overlooking the ocean.

What felt fine on a sunny summer afternoon made me sob uncontrollably on a dark night. A dark night of the soul. It made me question everything. What the hell was I doing here?

I had always dreamt about living off the grid – being connected to the land, the earth, and the sky in ways that are impossible to achieve in a suburb or big city. I thought that WAS my dream. To someone looking on I guess it would be no surprise that living it was something else.

I know I'm a wimp. When I reflect on it, I am deeply and profoundly embarrassed. However, I wouldn't be telling the truth if I didn't reveal what a sook I really am.

Sue had been completely satisfied with the hermit lifestyle. I wanted electricity and water and heat. Absence of these common features made me realize how much I took them for granted.

I know there are many people besides me around the world who enjoy a "back to grassroots lifestyle." It's just been more of a shock to my system than I had anticipated.

What was a mere inconvenience during a week or month-long stay, turned into a heart-wrenching crisis of faith in my very ability to exist, let alone thrive.

I hadn't intended on living like a monk in a monastery, depriving myself of what I had come to define as the most basic human need.

I still loved to cook and eat. I loved my glasses of wine in the evening, sitting by a warm fire. With a combination of some upgrades and improvements and the choice that I had made to live with some deprivation, the dream truly has delivered as imagined.

For example, gardening has been an even bigger thrill than I had imagined. It's taken a few years to learn some details, like just how much you need to cover everything to protect things from Sue's roaming horses or frost or the wild animals at night.

The hungry beasties seem to bite a chunk off any uncovered plant, especially the ones you want to keep. At first, I couldn't understand why all the successful gardens I saw were fully enclosed with wire mesh around the sides and over the top.

I thought it was overkill until I saw how much damage the animals create. The deep satisfaction that comes from eating complete meals with food picked just moments before eating can't be overstated.

Because I was into permaculture gardening in New Jersey, I had been building a food forest along the front lawn of my suburban home. As it turns out, this was great preparation for learning how to live off the grid.

Learning to use water carefully by creating optimum soil conditions and planting varietals where they could best survive with little to no added water is something I worked with in the States as well.

Primarily, the difference is that the native Australian varietals that do well in these conditions are new to me. They're still exotic and unfamiliar.

As we build a new native Australian food forest along the driveway, I learn something new every day. The best part about most of the varietals we've planted over the past few months is that the birds love them, while the Wallabies, wombats, and possums leave them alone.

Sue had done a fabulous job over the years, creating a haven for native Australian varietals and the iconic Waratah flowers. Her massive planting efforts have created giant hedges ringing the house and a magic climate for exotic birds of all types and intricate floral displays.

We just got our first few jars of honey from the honeybees that went in the first part of January. We made the hive ourselves during a class with a local beekeeper.

Watching it all come full circle has been an extreme pleasure. I don't usually even like honey. This honey isn't too sweet, has very complex floral notes, and carries the added flavor of having been homegrown. It all combines to make me appreciate honey all the more.

At the other end of the spectrum, the shock of living with limited electricity after four to five days of rain is still a massive strain on my ability to not freak out.

Even though we've upgraded the solar panels, upgraded the battery storage and more, there still comes a time when we can't live like "normal" people and just turn on the lights.

Back in the "normal universe," the first snap of cold weather or a deep snowstorm is fun as you sit by the fire and do nothing. Here, after an extended stretch of dreary rain, the electricity fails.

Then, when I most want to leap out of my skin and do nothing but eat popcorn and binge-watch something on Netflix, the answer is: "Oh, sorry, the batteries are down, we'll have to use candles tonight."

No TV. No bright reading light. I don't know if you've tried reading by candlelight, but it's a pain in the ass. Then, of course, there is the added fear of burning down the house if you fall asleep and screw up.

The beautiful things, the unexpected and the challenging.

In his book about the "Walden experiment," Thoreau tells us, "I learned this, at least, by my experiment: that if one advances confidently in the direction of his dreams, and endeavors to live the life which he has imagined, he will meet with a success unexpected in common hours."

Through all the challenges, disappointment, sorrow, and joy, I can finally begin to see the materialisation in my own life of this truth.

CHAPTER 19

Aussie, Aussie, Aussie

Aussie, Aussie, Aussie... Oi, Oi, Oi!

I thought it was a joke when I first heard the call. It seemed like a wounded animal cry gone wrong. What could it possibly mean?

I still don't know.

I may be put on some arcane watch list by the government for my ignorance in saying that.

"What?" I can't understand half of what the average Aussie farmer is saying. Worse yet are the Aussie jokes. Most of them are completely inexplicable to me. Even after someone's explained it, I still don't get it.

Even when someone patiently tries to explain it to me, I've still got a perplexed look on my face, trying to get a hint as to what they're talking about. Forget about laughing.

Aussie culture is a complete mystery to me. Growing up as an American, we have our own peculiar explanations for the events of history.

We were taught about the sacred "American Revolution" from the earliest school days. Almost every historical reference somehow links back to our revolution, throwing out the British and being released from their yoke: The Flag, The Constitution, Freedom and The Bill of Rights.

Watching the Aussies react to the concept of revolution is funny. "I don't get it, how is it that you still have a queen? From another country, no less." "Are you a country?" I don't get this whole Commonwealth thing.

What possible advantage is there in having a queen? How do you maintain a democracy with a queen and privileged landed nobles? I know there are many examples of this across Europe, but still; to me, it seems like nonsense.

The politics are weird but fascinating. They have mandated voting. I really like that. Everyone <u>has</u> to contribute their two cents. You can vote with a blank vote or a null vote, but you have to vote. If you're over 18 and don't vote, you'll get a fine in the mail a few days after the election.

While they have two main parties, the Liberals and Labor, up to a dozen other parties had candidates elected to State Government. Parties with names like Australian Recreational Fishers Party, Christian Democratic Party, Renewable Energy Party and The Greens. I like that there are so many different political parties that aim to champion single cause agendas.

I got a good laugh the other day. My brother asked me about the label on a bottle of wine he purchased. It's called "Insurrection." It's produced in Australia by one of the largest U.S. manufacturers using cheap Aussie grapes and is clearly designed to appeal to the American buyer.

The language on the label is a typical example of how Australians are portrayed in America: "Rise up against ordinary flavors and domesticated wines. Break free. Take a stand for concentrated pleasure and life on the edge. Rich, full-bodied Insurrection comes from Australia, where people decide for themselves, and no one apologises for living full throttle."

Marketing hype or not, my experience has taught me that it's true. Most Aussies do like to decide for themselves and live life to the fullest.

At the same time, there's a deep current of community here that I've never found in the States. Maybe that's because I never lived in a town of 600 people, or any rural, isolated area.

It feels like there's something more to it. Here in the middle of the heartland of Tasmania, the sense of connectedness and doing good things for the community remains a large and vibrant part of life.

Everyone volunteers for something, and most people volunteer for many things, partly from necessity. There just aren't enough people to get everything done and provide the level of services that exist here.

However, part of it goes beyond that. There is another element, part of the fabric of the people and the culture. I think it's infected me, and I like that.

CHAPTER 20

Volunteers

"I'm just going to take myself off methadone while I'm here on your property over the next two weeks. I hope that's OK with you," said Frankie, our newest volunteer.

We were in shock and mumbled something or other like, "Aaah, no. Not really".

I talked about the great volunteer spirit that exists in the community. In our case we have had so many fantastic volunteers come through the property to help us build the yurts, a teepee, create events, clear trails through the forest and many other things.

Twenty-two acres of land requires a lot of work. There is always too much to do such as moving logs, chopping up firewood, building fences, and doing all kinds of maintenance on the property.

This was the first time we had someone come as a volunteer without letting us know in advance what kind of help and support they were looking for in exchange for room and board.

Helping someone get off a methadone program after a heroin addiction was far beyond the skill set we possessed. There was no way we could provide that kind of support.

We were panicked. The only heroin addicts I ever knew were dead.

My mind flashed back to when I was 25 years old. I went to the morgue in Paris with my cousins to identify the body of another cousin who died of an overdose. By the time we arrived to identify the body, he had already turned some shade of green.

We got the report three days earlier, but we weren't allowed to see him until they finished the autopsy. That's an image I will never forget. I was one month older than my cousin, who was now lying on the steel morgue table, his lifeless eyes staring at the ceiling.

I had gone to Paris to spend time with my cousins before my daughter was born. I was newly married, had finished my winemaker training, and my life was full of hope.

When I saw him in the morgue, I was even more grateful for the opportunity and the life I was creating. I was in complete shock to know that my cousin has been "using."

Coming back to the present, I considered what little I knew. I had heard that methadone addiction following a heroin addiction is not uncommon. I had also heard that this addiction could be terribly destructive. I knew that highly qualified professionals with experience in this area were required.

In the spirit of community, we didn't want to give up. Within 48 hours, we had arranged for alcohol and drug rehabilitation counselors, who found Frankie a pharmacist, and medical doctors and worked out a treatment plan.

Frankie arranged to move to the local hotel and pub in town, and we agreed to let him come to the property to work during the day. Being on the land is quite healing. At night he would be in town if he needed immediate support.

All of this seemed fine – but that one little glitch is always the fly in the ointment.

Frankie was set to move into a house-sitting arrangement next to the pharmacy. However, there was one night that Frankie couldn't be housed at the pub and the house-sit wasn't ready yet, so we agreed to have him stay on the property for one night.

He arrived at our place in tears, saying, "I don't ever want to take methadone again. I'm stopping all of it right now." Frankie wanted to go cold turkey and not follow the recommendations of his counsellors or doctors.

There may be people who quit methadone cold turkey, but given the nature of the drug and Frankie's 13, or more, years of addictions, I was scared.

Within 24 hours he freaked out and was taken to the hospital in Launceston to get treatment. Luckily no one was injured, and Frankie was able to get into a formal rehab program with medical supervision.

The only remaining signs of Frankie's visit were the large burn marks where he decided to add new fire pits closer to the caravan he was staying in.

That experience provided many funny stories once it was over. Frankie was a charming and likeable character, even in his ungrounded state.

We quickly amended our volunteer policies and sign-up process to make sure there was a match between their needs and their ability to provide volunteer service.

One wonderful group of volunteers came through a woman Sue met at one of Australia's Council of Grandmothers events. They were in the middle of a life-changing move and wanted time to reflect before they jumped ahead, sold the house, and started a new life.

> *"What is the path to enlightenment?*
> *Chop wood and carry water.*
> *What is the path after enlightenment?*
> *Chop wood and carry water."*

This saying really hits home when you live off the grid and chop wood, and notice how high the water tank is every day.

Transformation and healing can come when people spend time connecting to the land and nature by doing simple routine chores – like chopping wood, gardening and paying attention to the amazing bounty of nature.

Karen was 52 and had some emotional challenges in dealing with a new relationship. She was seeking understanding about what she wanted to do with her life, how best to support her children and focus on her new love.

This seemed like familiar territory. I had gone through my own divorce, setting up a new life, and learning how to be myself again after 50. Her partner Scott was 59, and an experienced electrician.

His beautiful house was far away from where Karen's children lived. That was one challenge; also, there was the inevitable emotional baggage from previous relationships. The story is always the same.

These volunteers spent a month digging, gardening, creating paths on the property, adding solar panels to the shed and stabilising the solar panels on the caravan to run the electricity on the unit.

This simple work, done with their hands, provided the setting for an amazing transformation, both for them individually and together as a couple.

As they had time to sit, think, and chat, they were completely released from the need to do, or be or become anything. They simply allowed their thoughts to evolve naturally.

Watching them blossom as they connected more and more with the earth, the sky, their deep inner feelings and each other was a precious experience.

Another couple wanted to check out the place after seeing the sign off the main road. We agreed on an exchange of volunteer work time for a crystal healing for them that afternoon.

They were on an adventure, traveling across Australia, finding work along the way and camping in their Pajero truck that had a mega rooftop tent they pulled out each night.

Emma was a 33-year-old schoolteacher from the Netherlands. She quit her job over a year previously to travel the world. She had already been in Australia for over a year.

She met Tom on her journey, a 33-years-old IT professional. As a result, Tom was inspired to quit his job in Sydney and take to the road.

The afternoon they spent was so enjoyable they promised to

come back again on their next loop. They were off to pick cherries in Hobart the next morning.

We were thrilled to have them for those few hours. They were energetic and capable and somehow managed to do more work in that one afternoon than the previous group of volunteers had done in a week.

All these, and many more inspired and inspiring people have come through the property and helped us with the incredible amount of physical labor required to keep the forest at bay. Left alone, it wouldn't take long for the vegetation to completely overtake the house and gardens.

All this work is really a vehicle to allow us the opportunity to embrace the earth and touch the sky. To connect our souls to the power below us, and the invitations that beckon from above.

CHAPTER 21

Dunneys or Longdrops... Hmmm

Holding events for large groups of 30 or 40 people has some unexpected challenges. Especially when the event site is off-grid like we are. For example, how does everyone use the restroom?

The main house has a septic tank and a regular flushable toilet. Just one. The area around the yurts where the groups gather has two outhouses. In "Aussie-speak" that would be the dunnies.

I've gone back and forth about whether to call them "dunnies," or "longdrops." Both sound pretty graphic compared to "outhouse." Ah, well, there are bigger things to worry about.

We <u>are</u> in the process of fundraising to install composting toilets that don't involve large holes in the ground. They work almost exactly like normal toilets and still don't damage the landscape or require major excavation or permits from the local government.

Friends visiting from Canada helped us build outhouse frames to surround the longdrops. Strong winds have blown them over-- twice. Fortunately, no one was inside.

They were blasted to bits. Each time we rebuilt them with longer and stronger steel. We now have 5-foot steel poles driven into each of the four corners to anchor them down. Even with that, one of them leans like the Tower of Pisa from a massive wind storm.

Seeing how rectangular shapes get ruined by the wind, it makes me appreciate the canvas yurts. These have managed to withstand gale force winds of 100–150 k/h with nary a pickup.

To further accommodate our large events, we've added prefab units with showers. They collect the rainwater off the roof. That water is stored in a 1000 liter square container. Solar panels on the roof feed a battery that powers the electronic ignition to an instant gas water heater.

It's amazing how much support you need to create even such a simple system. Our guests have the opportunity to bathe in pure rainwater. It has been exciting for us to have the entire property supplied by collected rainwater.

The rectangular water units have also suffered major havoc from the strong winds. The doors were blown off and scattered around the property. Fortunately, the damage was limited by the cement foundations.

I have come to truly appreciate the round form of the yurt that was handcrafted by a local artisan. We were his first attempt at making these outdoor tent spaces for resale. Lucky us, we were his #1 paying client.

As it turns out, maybe we were not so lucky. The construction process itself was a big challenge. The builder was using amazing local hardwoods and sewed the ultra-thick sailboat canvas by hand for the exterior.

There were still real gaps in our knowledge about how to grade the floor to make sure the water drained out and did not flow into the yurt. And then there were the doors. The artisan said he was only putting in the walls, the windows, and the new plexiglass centerpiece. "I don't make doors," he informed. Yeah, except it's not really a secured space if there are no doors.

He did finally make us some doors and they've been fully functional and workable. If we do this again, I will definitely go with a prefab unit from a trusted supplier — one more steep learning curve in our adventure.

Because of the energetic nature of the land itself, the circular space of the yurt creates a magical cocoon of energy. This cocoon is highly conducive to connecting everyone who is inside the room. There's no hanging back in the corners or being left out.

The result is a phenomenal space for events that provides a natural feeling of connection and togetherness. We have been able to use it as a workspace for Sue's massage therapy, in addition to events and retreats.

The passive solar capacity of the roof on the yurt has been a wonderful bonus. Even on the coldest of days in the middle of winter, if the sun is shining, the yurt is toasty warm without any additional heating.

We've been learning to adapt and use what we have as the journey unfolds before us.

More additions have come as we have grown in our capacity to serve others and expand our own learning about sustainable living and being off the grid. Additional batteries, more solar panels, more water storage tanks, new fencing with better gates and even a wind turbine now grace the property.

We also have a new path through the woods to more easily gain access to sites where the power emanates from the earth.

Even with all these additions, everything on the property is, and always has been, completely off the grid. As exotic and interesting as this might sound, it significantly multiplies the complexity of the planning and operation of events.

Food storage, showers, bathrooms, safety concern, and a host of other things have come from our crash course in creating this dream.

My friend Senna, who takes groups on wilderness hiking trips here in Tasmania, has helped a lot with advice and practical help. For example, she taught me to freeze everything in advance and take it out of the freezer the day I need the food.

That way, I can be confident about food for a large group. This trick also allows me to have lots of extra food ready when a group turns up unexpectedly. The freezer lives in town at the post office. That means it is ON the grid where it has permanent electricity. We don't want to lose the contents when one of the extended rainstorms drains the batteries and leaves us in the dark.

CHAPTER 22

The Laurel Tree

One of the extraordinary living things on the property is the laurel tree. Over 20 feet tall and nearly 50 feet long, this laurel tree plays a symbolic and majestic role on the property.

It may not make sense that I describe a tree as 50 feet long, so let me explain. It was an average sized tree when Sue bought the property twenty-three years ago. The growth has been extraordinary. It has expanded in all directions until it now holds a dominant spot on the property.

To me, the tree seems somewhat mystical in its properties. It feels like a metaphor for life itself. As the tree grows, the canopy touches the ground and puts down roots where it touches. This means that the footprint of the tree is many times that of the main trunk itself.

From the outside, this massive living organism looks almost solid. You cannot see inside the canopy because the foliage is so thick. Only the tangled roots and branches are visible from the outside.

On the other hand, if you go inside the canopy and look out from the middle, you can see everything outside quite clearly. Somehow, the thick foliage is easy to see through.

So from the outside looking in, you see almost nothing and from the inside looking out, you see everything. It reminds me of the neural network in the brain.

Standing in it feels like you are in the brain of the tree looking out. Also, from the inside, you see the tangled mass of branches. That reinforces the brain metaphor because it looks like illustrations you might have seen of all the brain's intertwined neurons.

The evergreen leaves of this tree create a lush yet hushed environment. It feels like another world.

Another amazing thing about this tree is how quickly and vigorously new shoots spring out, even when large sections show decay. It reminds me a bit of my own body. Some parts are much weaker than they used to be, and yet, I still keep trying new things.

This tree continues to send out new shoots as the old thick branches become more fragile and break off. The new branches set down roots and hold up the entire space overhead like a giant umbrella.

We've cut an entrance to make it easy to get inside the canopy. The growth is so quick that we must prune this every year to maintain an easy path to the center of the tree.

There in the center, the giant ancient trunk creates a clearing the size of a big room. The setting feels like you are almost inside a cave filled with amazing treasures and secrets.

I'm sure the old tree still has many secrets to reveal. However, the magic of connecting with the life force of the tree is felt by all who are fortunate enough to experience that space.

CHAPTER 23

Every Time, It's a Miracle

Cindy was pregnant. Cindy is our horse. We had been getting up every night between 2 and 3 AM to monitor how the pregnancy was progressing. Of course, it was taking forever.

This was the longest horse pregnancy ever.

We didn't know the date of conception, so we had no estimate for when the foal would arrive. Cindy was a rescue horse that was so malnourished when Sue brought her home, her ribs were poking out, in addition to her noticeable "baby bump."

I'm quite sure a veterinarian would snicker at the use of that term, but as a mom, it works just fine. This all added to the uncertainty and the drama as the due date approached.

By September, after Cindy had been with us for some time, it was still hard to tell when the little one would come because Cindy is half Clydesdale. That horse breed, made famous by Budweiser beer commercials, is big and chunky. Since she was only half, Cindy was big, but not that big.

When I finally saw the little brown pile of legs and beautiful eyes peering at me from the paddock, tears welled up, unbidden, in my eyes. The new foal had gently landed on the soft grass and showed his face to the world.

I cried tears of joy at the birth of each of my children. Witnessing, once again, the miracle of new life brought me a similar feeling. Thankfully, this time, with a lot less pain.

I was overwhelmed with a renewed sense of how miraculous new life is, and the simple yet profound joy that accompanies the birth of a new being. We named the little guy Shiloh.

Watching this new soul, who was barely two feet tall to start with, learn to walk within a few hours of birth, was another miracle. At four months, Shiloh was nearly as tall as his mother. I guess that is because of the Clydesdale stud, which was the father half of the equation.

What I didn't realize at the time was just how powerful the emotions would be as we watched Shiloh begin to experience the world. The ever-changing journey brought up happy and sad memories of the first horse, Mika; Sue had lost a year earlier.

I had no idea how much depression and sadness remained hidden in our hearts, waiting to be triggered and pulled back into our emotional present as the weeks and months went by.

Mika had been a big horse, another Clydesdale. She had a giant personality and a twinkle in her eye. She had died suddenly of colic. Something had blocked her digestive system in such a way that we could not make her better. Her sudden death left us gasping for emotional air.

We tried everything we knew to save her and nothing had worked. We called the vet. His hour drive to come to the rescue seemed like an eternity.

He gave Mika injections to try to clear whatever was blocking her intestines and making it difficult for her to breath. Watching the pain and suffering in the horse's eyes as she struggled with every breath was heartbreaking.

Just a few hours earlier, Mika had been happy and lively as normal. I just couldn't accept that this sudden ailment could not be cured with modern medicine. Everything we did was to no avail.

Finally, Sue said, "She's about to die."

"What? How is that possible? She's still walking," I replied.

I guess that demonstrated how little I knew about horses. My lifelong experience was quite limited. I'd ridden them on trails on occasion, but I'd never owned or cared for a horse. I had certainly never lived with a horse that interacted with me like she was my best friend.

The entire community loved Mika. She was well known because she often stayed in a pasture right by the main road through Elephant Pass. Neighbors and tourists alike would often stop to give her an apple or a carrot, and she rewarded them with generous, friendly interaction.

Sue had gone to feed Mika her evening meal. I could see that something was making Mika struggle with her breathing, but I had no idea that this was a prelude to something life-threatening.

As part of her amazing past, Sue had been a jockey and worked for many years as a horse trainer, so I assumed she would easily be able to take care of whatever this was.

Sue called urgently and asked me to come to the paddock. When I got there, she simply said, "We need beer."

A bit dumbfounded, I said, "What? That'll take at least half an hour for me to drive to town, wait in line at the pub and get back up the hill."

"Too late," Sue responded. "She could be dead by then."

The urgency of the situation was slowly sinking into my consciousness and I suddenly remembered my friend across the street. I didn't think she was a beer drinker but I knew she had recently hosted a group of family and friends. Maybe they had some beer left over. It was worth the phone call.

I quickly made a phone call and asked what might've sounded like a strange question: "Do you have any beer? Our horse Mika is in trouble and Sue says the answer is beer."

None of this made any sense to me, but I was going to do everything I could to find beer because Sue was insistent.

It sounds crazy, but moments later, there we were trying to pour beer down Mika's throat. As you can imagine, it was pretty complicated, trying to get the beer into the horse. Most of the beer went onto Sue's head and all over me, but nobody noticed.

With hindsight and explanation, I realise that the carbonation bubbles in beer help release the spasms in a horse's bowel, however; it has no effect if the colic comes from a blocked or twisted bowel.

Mika's playful habit of rolling around on the ground like a puppy might have been fun for her and amusing for people to watch, but it's not a good thing for their digestive tract.

We got as much of the beer in her as we possibly could, and then Sue slowly walked her from the paddock back to our property. The walk was a short 3 kilometers, but with the struggling horse, it took a very long time.

Her head was nearly touching her knees as she struggled with the slow walk back home.

By the time we got there, the veterinarian had arrived. He gave Mika an injection to help with the colic and to help clear the blockage. Sue kept Mika moving at a slow walk.

She did not want the horse to stop moving and lay down for fear that she would never get up again.

After a few hours, I think it was near midnight; the veterinarian said there was nothing more he could do for her. It was obvious it was over. Sue made the heart-wrenching decision to put an end to Mika's suffering.

Living out in the country, away from the hustle and limited experiences of the city, you get exposed to life and death in the animal world more often and more powerfully.

People raise chickens and eat them. When you do that, you realize what's on that meat tray you buy in the supermarket. There's a much clearer link to the food you eat and the animals we play with.

Some people raise chickens and give them to friends because they don't want to eat them. Others only raise chickens for their eggs. In the end, it's all really the same thing.

We have a big dog that is a mix between a blue heeler and a kelpie. He regularly kills wallabies and brings them back to his little sister, a small fluffy ball of fur. Life and death is part of the same cycle.

Because the animals around us die on a regular basis, we try to lose our attachment to them, but this horse was special to us, and her passing was both painful and unexpected.

The day after her death, Mika was going to pull two of our very good friends in a carriage to make a magnificent entrance for their wedding party. Mika had been practicing for months and had learned how to pull the old-fashioned wooden wheel carriage gently.

Instead, we watched as a giant machine made a great hole in the earth to bury our beloved Mika. Even though the hole was covered up, it left a great emptiness in our hearts.

The arrival of the new foal, Shiloh, gave us a new opportunity to rejoice in life and stop feeling the depression of death.

CHAPTER 24

Mom's Dementia

I expected that the biggest challenge of moving over 10,000 miles away from my kids and my family would be the separation from the kids. I just couldn't see how the relationships would stay vibrant and exciting.

When I first moved, my son was working for City Year, which is a non-profit educational foundation in Boston. My daughter was in Edinburgh, Scotland, studying to be a veterinarian. Neither of these is close to New Jersey, and nobody was going to pop over for dinner. Still, Boston was only a few hours away from New Jersey, and I had traveled to Scotland, it didn't seem that far. When I moved to Tasmania, they suddenly felt like billions of miles and time zones away.

Of course, nothing is ever as you expect. The biggest challenge was the helplessness and distance I experienced as I watched my mother's mental health slowly deteriorate, and then, as I tried to help in the action required for her future care.

For me, keeping contact and maintaining relationships over the years has often consisted of a daily text, picture, email, quick phone call, or some other digital connection. It was fast and easy and surprisingly personal. The goal for my mom was to have a phone call once a week.

I had always been a traveler. I think I was the first child to take off from the nest and move far away. My first trip abroad was when I was 19. I was a sophomore at Georgetown, and I spent a six-month semester at the American University in Cairo.

I think that's what happens when you're from a big family. Either there is some degree of a "cookie-cutter" nature from one kid to the next, or you're all completely different.

Our family came down on the side of each child being completely different and fiercely independent.

While in Egypt, I sent many postcards and those thin tissue paper airmail letters home to keep everybody up to speed.

Thirty years later, my parents were preparing to move to Florida from the old homestead in New Jersey. As we dug through piles and piles of boxes to get ready for the change, to my surprise, I found a whole box full of my Egyptian correspondence.

Wow, I had not expected that. I was pleased but also surprised that anyone would have kept those things.

Right after college, I went to France for a year to study French. Like sometimes happens, one year turned into seven, and I returned home to my parents' house in New Jersey with a French husband and two young children.

However, there was no surprise because I had kept in touch with monthly telephone calls. When I think about how easy and inexpensive it is today to keep in touch by one of half a dozen methods, I am grateful.

Funny thing though, it still seems like a hard thing to do for some people. I guess it's not the technology after all.

It was almost imperceptible at first, little things like the frequent repetition of the same story, accompanied by the inevitable question, "Did I tell you this already?"

"Yeah, Mom, you did." In quiet moments, when I was honest with myself, I could see it; it scared me, and I knew it was not going to get better.

Then came the big changes, one after another. Within one year, I became concerned that she was living alone, even though one of my brothers was a mere 15-minute drive away.

My brother, who lived closest, had always been on call for every emergency. However, even being on call didn't mean that he always had control of the car keys and knew everything that was going on, or might be going on in the house.

She didn't want to give up driving.

I decided to start calling my mom daily. It turned out to be easier said than done because she has had the challenge of learning to use an iPhone with dementia.

Even though we all take our smartphones for granted, I still find myself confused about which buttons to push for what, and how to make things work, especially when the operating system changes frequently.

Even worse, I am completely flummoxed when I have to borrow Sue's android phone. I can't figure out how to even make a phone call.

I guess it's not that much of a surprise that my mom hasn't yet figured out how to use her iPhone very well. They could probably make a "senior's edition," with a giant keypad for easy phone dialing and giant app buttons on the home screen.

Now there's an idea worth some cash.

It seems crazy easy until I think about what's really involved. Besides simply making phone calls, what about questions like How do you charge the phone? How do you even tell if it needs charging? How do you create an awareness of what the phone is capable of?

After you get used to your chosen smartphone, it's easy, but to a neophyte, it's not at all obvious what to swipe when to tap and what to do to start or end a call.

Mom came from a time when a landline was her primary tool. She rarely uses her iPhone, and I can't remember ever seeing her use it voluntarily.

I don't know; maybe this iPhone stuff is wishful thinking. When the time comes, the answer could be to go back to a trusted landline when she moves into an assisted living facility.

At least half of the time when I call, she picks up says, "Hello, hello" and then hangs up. She feels confounded that she can't hear me.

I usually try two or three times. Sometimes I'm fast enough to say, "Don't touch any buttons, Mom!" So we can chat; otherwise, I wait till the next day and try again.

Because I was talking to her so often, it was easy for me to notice the progression of her condition. She was slowly losing her memory, one of the key indicators of advancing dementia.

A few weeks ago, Mom had an "incident." She fell unconscious at the dinner table while out with my brother's family and friends.

That night was scary and serious. She had to be resuscitated and remain in the hospital overnight for observation. They found no signs of a stroke or heart disease, but there had been a sharp downward turn in her short-term mental capacity.

The silver lining was that it mobilized my brothers and her medical caregivers to realize that she shouldn't be driving. Did I just say that? Holy shit, she was occasionally driving before that? It was time to act.

We'd been trying for years to get my mother to move out of her house and into my brother's place. Two and a half years ago, I thought we finally had her convinced. The plan was to have her move into his home while a separate apartment unit was built in his backyard.

I had flown to Florida from Australia over Christmas, and we set up meetings with the real estate agent, cleaned out the garage, gave dozens of boxes to charity and figured out who wanted what of the furniture and other possessions. All this was done to reduce the size of the move.

Then nothing, total radio silence. Mom had decided she didn't want to move. She was perfectly fine where she was and all progress on getting her to stay with my brother halted.

She decided to wait until the new unit was fully complete before she did anything about moving. This was a terrible scenario because building the unit had turned into a nightmare.

The plans never made it to council approval. There was always one more issue with the water lines, the sewer lines; or the architect needed another revision. There were endless delays for the small one-bedroom unit.

As this all unfolded, I was worried that she would get in the car, forget where she was going and get into an accident, or leave the stove on, or who knows what else.

In the end, the building of the unit was scrapped, and we got her to move in with my brother. That was a short-term solution. It quickly became clear that she was going to need more care than he could provide, in case another "incident" occurred.

Getting Mom to leap independence to an assisted facility turned out to be another complicated journey. There were a lot of phone calls, many personal visits, and endless worry.

Even after deciding she had to get to a facility, there was an enormous amount of discussion between siblings about where she should be. We eventually decided that she would move to Houston.

That was preferable to Fort Lauderdale since three of my brothers live in the Houston area. That means less pressure on any one person when things get difficult.

I am truly grateful that none of the doomsday scenarios played out. We found her a safe, very fancy, assisted living unit complete with pool, monitoring systems in the units and all the facilities on one floor.

It's difficult to watch this happen to a parent. I was a witness to my mother's stress as she dealt with my father's Alzheimer's for seven years while he lived at home.

Even with the support of expert caregivers; it was an enormous strain on her. Her dementia seems only to limit her short-term memory at the moment, but I don't know what's coming.

I thoroughly rejoice in the fact that there are people who provide genuine care in an assisted living environment.

During all this time, I was reading David Hawkins, *Letting Go*. One chapter talks about loved ones experiencing the loss of faculties and illness as a sign for us to let go of our attachment to them.

It is our time to gently say goodbye as they transition to the next stage of their life. This whole process was difficult and draining, especially from the other side of the world.

CHAPTER 25

Sleepless Nights

I was out like a light after an entire week of sleepless nights. The stress and emotion of the previous days had completely done a number on me.

The plane rocked gently on the 15-hour flight from Los Angeles to Melbourne, and I was happy to get nearly seven hours of uninterrupted sleep. The other hours I gratefully sat in silence with my thoughts.

Six days earlier, not even the comfort of a business class seat allowed me to sleep on the trip to Houston.

After all the calls, emails, persuading, worry, and all of the rest of it, I was finally on the way to participate in getting my mom into the facility we had chosen.

I balled my eyes out watching the movie "Lion," as Dev Patel left Tasmania to find his mother in India.

I was anxious and worried about what I would feel coming face-to-face with my mom, to witness her anxiety about what was happening to her mind and her body. I expected it would also be difficult to help her face the fears of the big move.

My brother Tim picked me up at the airport, and we went straight to my mom's new "apartment" at the Village in the Woodlands. It was an impressive sight and looked more like a boutique hotel than an assisted living facility.

We surrounded Mom with family, my brother Dave and niece Rachel, as well as new beautiful furniture. I think Rachel is currently my mom's best friend and, at the age of 19, she shows amazing care and concern for my mother that I've rarely witnessed between generations.

Rachel was the rock to ground, my mom, as they flew from Fort Lauderdale to Houston. Her genuine smile and caring manner were a great comfort.

Rachel and Mom arrived the day before, and we expected her to move in on Friday. Of course, there was one more glitch that got in the way of keeping to the schedule we had planned.

The TB test results from the Florida doctor had not yet arrived, that meant she could not move into the facility. Eventually, that took care of itself, but not without creating one more little piece of stress.

On top of all of the technical, financial, and organizational things required for such a move, the stress was amplified because of the number of siblings involved, all whopping seven in all.

We lived all over the place, which meant that the distance was also a challenge. We had originally selected Florida but later transferred to Houston.

After more discussion, it made more sense to have just one move right into the Woodlands where she would be near the most family because three of her sons live in that area.

John had done all the heavy lifting in Florida for the past two years. Her recent stay of a couple of weeks at his house had created an additional emphasis around the truth; she needed much more attention and activity then we could provide. The real answer was the assisted living environment where we now stood.

Another bonus, my three brothers own a company in Houston that builds medical office buildings for doctors. They have created great relationships that would facilitate excellent care for Mom.

One immediate benefit was that the minute Mom landed she could get a complete physical and completed paperwork. The 48-hour delay around the TB test still had to happen, so Monday was the earliest possible day for her to move in.

Like every problem, the delay brought a benefit because it gave us all additional time together to enjoy some meals and a great barbecue. Some friends and my niece formed a group to create a feeling of real intimacy and connection. Having the three of us together with Mom felt very special.

The actual check-in process at The Woodlands Village was a pleasant experience. It made us feel great about our decision to have her stay there.

My brother Dave and I spent the day with Mom going through the activity schedule and getting her settled in. We all had lunch and dinner together.

There was a pullout couch, but I wanted my mom to experience me leaving and coming back, so she didn't feel completely dependent on me during the settling in process.

I had been forewarned that dementia patients often suffer a setback when they change environments. We saw that the previous year when she came along on two family vacations.

We saw it again at The Village. We assisted her to participate in events, which she seemed to enjoy actively.

On day two at the facility it was clear Mom didn't remember anything about the previous day. At least we could relax about her medication since we had turned that responsibility over to the facility. She was compliant, and that seemed to be going okay.

It was probably easier for her to take direction from the staff than one of her kids. On top of that, she saw all the other patients taking medication, which made it easier for her to go along.

One strong indicator of adjustment issues was her lack of appetite. We had to beg her to have even a small muffin for breakfast as she continually said she wasn't hungry.

Driving in a new city is challenging, even with a GPS. Mom and I went out shopping in the morning to get some supplies and materials to put some pictures on the walls.

Just like some bad movie script, I took a wrong turn and ended up driving three extra miles with a few loops around and around to get back to where I needed to be.

Mom had a little carsickness, which was turning into major distress. We decided to skip Michaels crafts store and go back to the apartment.

She seemed unsettled and queasy. She sat down and kept repeating, "I've never felt this bad before."

That pushed my guilt buttons, and I felt bad that I had caused this problem. We thought it might be side effects from the new medication.

Mom refused to touch her lunch because of the way she felt. Eventually, we got her to take a few sips of ginger ale, but that was it.

Over the previous few weeks, she had described feeling faint and experiencing dizziness along with expressing a desire to lose weight. I was afraid she was skipping meals.

On top of that, she couldn't remember which meals she ate and which she skipped. Missing this meal was not a good plan.

All this worry and concern left me feeling uneasy as well. As Mom started to enjoy the afternoon activities, my stomach settled down, and I began to get centered again.

My brother came in and announced that Mom was going to go for a walk with a group of residents led by Erica. Erika was a dynamic 90-year-old who was the local champion in motivating resident participation in activities.

Erica was doing something amazing by pushing the residents to walk without walkers and stay active and strong. She kept saying, "You need to be strong to be independent. What if there's a fire? You need to know how to get out of here on your own."

So, there was my mom, hobbling along ready to go out into the street to walk along the waterway. I quickly caught up to her and said she might want to wait for a day when she had eaten lunch, so she didn't have a fainting spell. However, I was excited that she wanted to go.

We changed the medication schedule for after breakfast, and that seemed to eliminate the problem. I also told my brothers it would probably be best not to take her for rides in the car until after lunch.

The professionals assured me that it would only take a few weeks for her to adjust to her new medication, and at least a month to adjust to the new facility. This made me feel a bit better.

There are some upsides to dementia. If you can't remember anything you did the day before, how could you ever carry around guilt and feel bad?

I love the fact that every morning, my mom would introduce herself. "Hi, I'm Ruth. I just got here last night. What's your name?"

By the end of the week, the residents were catching on and saying things like, "Hey, I already know you. You've been here before."

It was all in good spirits, and the patience and tolerance they exhibited were beautiful. I expect that this happened a lot. I was grateful for those residents there for physical reasons who could help those struggling with their memories.

All of this played through my mind more than once in between my sleep episodes on the flight home.

I was grateful it was done, even though I still have lingering concerns about the adjustment and whether I had done everything I could, or should do, to take care of my beloved mother.

CHAPTER 26

Struggle In Paradise

It's not possible. There I was procrastinating. Again.

With Mom settled, I expected that things would be easier, and I could get into creating the business I still imagined I wanted.

Something was still not right. I had come to immediately recognize the unsettled feeling of something not being in alignment.

As part of creating a coaching practice, I had committed to creating a high-end live event for elite business owners and executives.

When I started, I had two months to get it organized, and I thought, "no problem." My ego knew it could be a great way to kick off my Australian business.

This would allow me some local clients instead of having everything virtual in the U.S. or in Europe, where the massive time difference could be a problem.

It wasn't happening. A massive conflict was going on in my mind. My ego was resisting losing my long-standing identity as a wine expert, business expert, and someone who was a big dog in that field.

I began to realize that part of the conflict was that I had not yet answered a fundamental question: "Did I want to launch a whole new consulting and coaching business in Australia?"

Given my experience, my expertise, and my history, it made perfect sense. However, I was confronting the reality that I didn't know many people here, particularly in that capacity.

Most people in Tasmania know me as the meditation, intuitive healer, and stress elimination expert, not as a business mentor and coach.

I was feeling threatened. What if I couldn't do it? What if I didn't want to? I had committed to specific tasks and time targets to make the event happen, but, I just wasn't doing it. Part of me didn't want to.

My ego was loud and clear in its desire to keep my old identity and to keep cash flowing in Australia based on my years of expertise. The growing "heart-centered" side of me had other ideas.

As things stood, I was spending my free time walking in the woods, taking the dogs to the beach for a run, gardening, chopping wood, doing everything but focusing on meeting potential clients.

The fact that my three top venue choices were booked up and couldn't accommodate a large group didn't help. These places are phenomenal hotels along Freycinet and The Hazards, regularly rated in the top 10 global destinations. They offer stunning scenery and amazing accommodations.

The next step down in housing and venue space wasn't going to cut it. The whole thing was feeling more and more like a waste of time. On top of that, this entire battle was taking place in the quiet recesses of my heart and the noisy conversations in my head.

I was frustrated at myself for not wanting what could have been a very lucrative proposition. Moreover, I was furious with myself for not wanting what my brain said was a logical and great way to launch in Australia.

So so, I cried – as I had done so many times over the past few years.

Letting out all of the frustration, anger, sadness, and grief that came from the new truth, that my past life and past ambitions were dying. They were no longer part of me. Some part of me still desperately wanted to cling to that old me. I didn't want to let them go.

That old familiar self somehow didn't fit anymore. I was unsure how to resolve the business model with the life I was living in Tasmania and loving to the max.

This reminds me of the story of the Mexican fisherman, below.

> A vacationing American businessman standing on the pier of a quaint coastal fishing village in southern Mexico watched as a small boat with just one young Mexican fisherman pulled into the dock. Inside the small boat were several large yellowfin tunas. Enjoying the warmth of the early afternoon sun, the American complimented the Mexican on the quality of his fish.
>
> "How long did it take you to catch them?" the American casually asked.
>
> "Oh, a few hours," the Mexican fisherman replied.

"Why don't you stay out longer and catch more fish?" the American businessman then asked.

The Mexican warmly replied, "With this, I have more than enough to meet my family's needs."

The businessman then became serious, "But what do you do with the rest of your time?"

Responding with a smile, the Mexican fisherman answered, "I sleep late, play with my children, watch ball games, and take siesta with my wife. Sometimes in the evenings I take a stroll into the village to see my friends, play the guitar, sing a few songs…"

The American businessman impatiently interrupted, "Look, I have an MBA from Harvard, and I can help you to be more profitable. You can start by fishing several hours longer every day. You can then sell the extra fish you catch. With the extra money, you can buy a bigger boat. With the additional income that larger boat will bring, before long you can buy a second boat, then a third one, and so on, until you have an entire fleet of fishing boats."

Proud of his own sharp thinking, he excitedly elaborated a grand scheme which could bring even bigger profits, "Then, instead of selling your catch to a middleman you'll be able to sell your fish directly to the processor or even open your cannery. Eventually, you could control the product, processing, and distribution. You could leave this tiny coastal village and move to Mexico City, or possibly even Los Angeles or New York City, where you could even further expand your enterprise."

Having never thought of such things, the Mexican fisherman asked, "But how long will all this take?"

After a rapid mental calculation, the Harvard MBA pronounced, "Probably about 15-20 years, maybe less if you work really hard."

"And then what, señor?" asked the fisherman.

"Why that's the best part!" answered the businessman with a laugh. "When the time is right, you would sell your company stock to the public and become very rich. You would make millions."

"Millions? Really? What would I do with it all?" asked the young fisherman in disbelief.

The businessman boasted, "Then you could happily retire with all the money you've made. You could move to a quaint coastal fishing village where you could sleep late, play with your grandchildren, watch ball games, and take siesta with your wife. You could stroll to the village in the evenings where you could play the guitar and sing with your friends all you want."

The moral of the story is: Know what matters in life, and you may find that it is already much closer than you think.

I studied international finance at Georgetown University, and I was probably still in school when I first heard that story. My interpretation of it has dramatically shifted over the years. My initial reaction was, "Yeah! Build a big business!" Build it bigger!"

I was now that fisherman, AND AT THE SAME TIME, I was the fancy business consultant wanting to build a big business.

That psychic split in my brain was epic, alternating between the two personalities was wreaking havoc every single time I sat down at the computer to work. I was both.

However, I still didn't know which one would win.

I finally admitted to Kellan, my coach, I didn't want to do the event. Even though a few weeks earlier, I had been sure that I did. I felt silly saying that, but it was true.

It was time to completely let go of my old way of thinking and being.

Now I realize I've come full circle. I want to connect with the earth and sky. I want to relax and draw and paint. I want very much to help other people who are on a path to find their own way to renewing important connections in their lives.

*"I get paid for that now, was my response.
It was as simple as that."*

- Barbara Longue

PART III

Your Highest Self

CHAPTER 27

What's Next?

Transitions are always important and almost always scary.

Once I came to grips with the fact that I was not going to create the "big business" model I had expected, the obvious question was, "What now?"

Gratefully, I have the time and space in the life I have created to consider and answer that question carefully. This includes experimenting with all kinds of things to see what feels right.

This experimentation includes making mistakes, learning new things, making adjustments, and learning to live, love, and laugh along the way.

I'm learning not to tie my value and self-worth to the immediate success of something I put my hand to. What a glorious freedom.

I want to help others and perhaps be a light and guide to those seeking similar changes. Exactly what that would look like, I don't know yet.

Let's see what the next steps bring. No matter what that is. Like every step on this amazing journey, I am committed to moving ahead to see what else waits around the next corner.

This section describes what I have learned and implemented to become my highest self, for me and my family and friends no matter how far away they may be.

I will also share some examples of how I help other people work through the same issues.

How do _you_ make your life meaningful?

How do _you_ create sacred space inside your day, inside your head for all those deep connections that come from your biggest and best self?

One key piece for me was to finally recognize the truth and lies of the life I had been living. I then learned to live, accept, and surrender to the life I wanted to experience.

Sometimes we call those lies "stories." Maybe it softens the word, but they are false all the same. We all make up stories about why we can't do something, or about why it has to be so hard.

However, as you go with me through the next part of the journey, you will see that mostly this is stuff we make up. That means we can make it vanish just as quickly.

CHAPTER 28

A New Beginning

I think I felt like that brand-new foal we had welcomed into the family. The pressure was off.

What an <u>amazing</u> relief. I did not have to be or DO anything.

I was relieved and excited to have the space to BE myself and allow my story to come out.

Within 24 hours of knowing that I wanted to write THIS book, I had all the chapters mapped out, a plan for a membership site for the Vortex and an online course fleshed out.

It suddenly all made perfect sense and became incredibly easy to make massive progress quickly.

I had been struggling for three years between the conflict of my "old" self and my "old" life, and how to make it mesh with my new life.

I completely surrendered to the simple truth of fully living the life I'd chosen, and NOT trying to mesh the old with the new.

The conflict was gone. I felt relieved and ecstatic. I had made this giant transformation to lead a much simpler life, and I was completely in integrity with my new choices.

I had nothing to prove since I wasn't trying to hold onto the competitive and aggressive businesswoman that had been my old identity.

Finally, I was completely at peace being known as, "That person who lives in the middle of nowhere in a forest overlooking the ocean." That was enough.

I no longer needed the external validation that came from being paid by someone "because I was important." It was enough that I felt at peace and in power with my own daily choices about how I choose to live my life and create value and good for those around me.

I finally had a game plan that I could live with. Not someone else's goals or aspirations for me. My plan and it fit with my lifestyle of living as simply as possible.

I knew that I wanted to help other people connect to their true desire and bring deep meaning into their life, without having to leave their whole life behind.

I know many people who live off the grid and enjoy tiny house living, but they probably weren't going to be my main target audience.

I deeply wanted to support those people who feel overwhelmed, as I once did, with life racing by you as you power through all your daily activities. I wanted to help people feel alive again in their daily life.

To notice that true satisfaction and happiness does not come from the daily grind.

To notice that we have this ONE life we're living right now, and enjoyment and satisfaction mustn't be put off until "retirement," or until your next vacation, or until the weekend.

You can live your life now. Today. This very moment. Right now.

Let me say that again: Right here. Right now.

I often remember a freshman course at Georgetown given by a Jesuit priest. We spent three months discussing how people create sacred space in their profane existence. Many of those thoughts and words came from St. Augustine, and they are all about creating that sacred space of deep meaning. It's possible, even without ditching society and moving to a hilltop in the middle of nowhere or dropping out of everything to join a monastery or nunnery.

That sacred place lives within you. You have to learn to listen

YOU can create that space at any time of the day or night, to make it sacred and meaningful to you.

It comes from creating habits that include taking care of yourself, loving yourself enough to get a good night's sleep, or taking time with friends to enjoy life and relax.

You can start right now by taking the time to have an actual conversation with your spouse, not about the kids and not about the bills, but life and NOW and feelings.

Create habits that allow yourself to truly reconnect with your family, your loved ones, and most of all, yourself.

I realise that I did not run away from my life in New Jersey. I was drawn to be in this exact spot because of the energy emanating from the Vortex.

Maybe that's why it took me so long to get over who I was and what I did in my previous life. Whatever the reason, the journey was worth it.

I am incredibly grateful to the help and support that I've had from all those along the way in this journey--my family, my coach, and the amazing community here in the middle of Tasmania.

Winter is coming.

Be fearful.

Or not.

You get to choose what you wish to experience at this very moment. I choose to be fully present right here, right now.

"Enlightenment is not something that occurs in the future, after 50 years of sitting cross-legged and saying "OM." It is right here, in this instant."

– David Hawkins, Letting Go

CHAPTER 29

Case Study

Like most people, I'm sure you have felt stressed and overwhelmed at work, probably sometimes to the breaking point.

What do you do when your coworkers don't seem to have the same opinions, values, sensitivities, and other character traits that you do?

Here's a case study from my experience with a local business about how to handle these things.

I had led some successful meditation sessions and deep relaxation sessions with the city employees in the past. Given that success, when they had a new problem, they came asking for help.

The leadership team noticed that their employees had internal conflicts, bad morale, and other productivity robbing behaviors.

The leadership group had instructions from further up the chain to do something to create a more harmonious and productive workplace. Senior management also indicated they were ready to look for new solutions since what they were doing wasn't getting the results they wanted.

I sat down with senior management, had a conversation about the challenges they were facing. I wanted to make sure I understood what was happening and get some details.

In the course of the conversation, it became clear to me that a few more meditation sessions were not going to cut it. Employees were feeling overwhelmed by stress.

This feeling was wreaking havoc in the workplace. There were suggestions of possible bullying, and employees believed that coworkers and management weren't listening to their needs.

I use meditation a lot in my coaching, but I didn't think that meditation alone would be enough to create the breakthrough that was needed to spark a return to productivity and harmony.

We needed to tackle some more basic problems.

This assignment allowed me to create a complete program to eliminate stress at work. The goal was to create a better working environment for employees.

The key indicators for success would be less stress, less sick days, less gossip at the water cooler, and greater productivity while on the job. At the same time, we wanted them to feel empowered and have permission to be creative in solving workplace issues.

I was determined to get to the root of the problem and not just put on a Band-Aid.

I knew that eliminating stress would do all of those things.

They agreed to implement my 12-week program. We would meet once a week for 30 minutes before the start of the workday.

One initial goal was to create a safe place where employees could build a connection with each other. At the same time, they would learn and implement a series of practices and tools to eliminate the high-stress items that occurred every day.

Below is a link for you to take your workplace stress survey so you can understand how your workplace measures up. It's called the *Lifestyle Entrepreneur Quiz*.

http://bit.ly/BizQuizLE

One initial requirement was to come to a common understanding of the word "stress" itself. Although it is simply a word, it has come to take on a life of its own and generally means completely different things to different people.

The word "stress" as we use it today did not even have its current connotation until after 1936 when Austrian Hans Selyer used it to describe the overall effects of multiple stressors on the body.

Today we generically use that word all the time as a scapegoat for almost anything; this creates its own set of problems. Someone simply saying, "I'm stressed out," creates a stress reaction in others around them.

By creating a common definition and understanding, we began to see how the word is misused. We talked about how to identify the root of the issue that seems to be causing the problem.

Employees may have problems communicating what they want or reluctant to describe how they feel honestly. They may have problems caused by avoiding their problems.

The long and short of it is to encourage people to look honestly at what the actual problems are. By being honest and open, it is easier to see that all these problems have solutions.

Solutions to problems always come from a place of "higher consciousness" than the place we were in when we created the problem. That means we first needed to raise awareness in the group to understand what was happening.

I related a story about a man who was receiving threatening letters. He went to the police with these anonymous letters, and they began an investigation to see what was happening.

In the course of the investigation, the police learned that the man had been involved in an argument with nearly every business owner in the area. Also, the police couldn't find anyone who enjoyed speaking with this man.

With that new information, the likely cause, actions, and outcomes of the situation are different.

Is the problem the threatening letters or the seeming inability of the man to communicate effectively? Arguing with everyone you meet is not normal – there is a larger problem at play.

There were many such examples and stories throughout the class. Each story created a learning opportunity for growth.

Over the twelve weeks, the group members had the opportunity to practice what they were preaching. For example, one practice area that came up was not making fun of co-workers because they had different thoughts from your own.

There were more than 80 employees in the office. Nineteen signed up to take the course. Sixteen finished the 12 weeks. Two dropped out due to "lack of time." One left the firm.

It's a shame that two employees dropped out because they "didn't think they had enough time." One result of eliminating stress is that you become able to create the time you need to do what is truly essential.

Doing what's important, as opposed to simply being "busy." Everyone is busy today. Busy is the new stress marker.

However, busy has nothing to do with productivity.

Getting done what's most important, and learning to know what your BOSS thinks is most important is the real key to success.

Learning what level of quality is needed to call a job done.

Learning who needs to approve different parts of the project and who decides when the work is "good enough."

We examined why those who take the role of "perfectionist" create costs in business when absolute perfection may not even be desirable.

We looked at how to apply the "Pareto Principle," the 80/20 rule, as it applies to time allocation during the workday. This allowed them to get more done with less effort.

Over the twelve weeks, the workers showed a statistically significant reduction in stress levels and their ability to handle verbal communications with colleagues and clients. By all accounts, it was a great success.

Measuring again, twelve weeks after the end of the sessions, the human resources department was still noticing significant improvements and lower stress in the behavior of the workers who participated.

The senior management staff was also encouraged to attend. In the end, even the most skeptical found many good things happened during the 12-week course.

Most importantly, the biggest skeptics admitted that it helped them understand their colleagues much better, and it created more empathy among the team members.

Creating an efficient, productive workplace environment is more than simply offering flextime or health benefits. The improved atmosphere in this case study created long term effects. This provides a significant upside not just for employee morale, but also for company productivity and profit.

The company was so pleased with the success and productivity boost that came from the first 12-week session that they decided to do it again. They created an additional workshop so that more workers could attend, and an ongoing support series to make sure that the changes are grounded and permanent.

CHAPTER 30

Lies and More Lies

It's complicated when you look out at life and try to decide what is true. We all live with a set of perceptions based on what our associations and circumstances tell us is true. Usually, we accept these unwritten assumptions and frameworks without thinking.

We don't realise how many of the beliefs and assumptions we make every single day are based on stories, outdated truths, half-truths, and flat out lies.

Distortions.

Misconceptions.

Outright wrong ideas about everything.

> *Byron Katie says it best, "Question Everything."*
> *"Ask, is it true?"*

Ask this over and over again. The persistence of our misconceptions is crazy.

Let's think about a simple example. How about the beautiful sunrise and all those glorious pictures you took at the beach on vacation of the sun coming up over the ocean.

A lie. A mistake. A misunderstanding.

The sun doesn't "come up" anywhere. The sun does not move around our little planet. We, the Earthlings, reside on this planet as it moves around the sun. I use an obvious but small example to illustrate the point.

Think about how long humans believed the world was flat. The heretics who said otherwise were burned at the stake or had a stake driven through their heart. It was not safe to question commonly held truths, or supposed basic facts.

I'm stressed out.

Overusing the word stress is another example of a misconception or a lie. As I mentioned earlier, the use of this word wasn't even created until 1936 by Hans Selye, an Austrian living in Canada.

As is clear in his research, he didn't believe the word should ever be used to create a "thing." Instead, it was simply a description of an observed phenomenon.

Wow, we all sure missed that boat.

What you have are problems. The feeling that you can't solve or do anything about a problem may create a physical reaction. Then we focus on the "stress." Then we try to manage that.

Instead, if you begin to analyze, review, and become aware of what your actual problems are, you can begin to look at everything from a completely new perspective. You don't have stress; what you do have are stories.

Here's another big fat lie: You have to keep up with the Jones'.

It's another powerful misconception, a messy lie with ugly consequences.

Who even told you who the Jones' were? Where did you get that?

Maybe you got it growing up. Maybe it came from real or imagined pressure from your colleagues at work, or maybe your country club.

Most people have some image of what it means to be "normal." Some definition of what you're supposed to want, supposed to have, supposed to be --house, car, closet, you know the drill.

Marketers have been perfecting the process of figuring out your hot buttons for decades. That's how they get you to buy their stuff over and over again, whether you need it or not.

Not just any product. You must have their specific product – their car, or house, or whatever. Never mind the finances. Go right ahead. Go even further into debt. That's more important than anything. Ignore the fact that housing prices are ridiculous and don't correlate with salaries, or economic conditions, or anything else. Just keep up with those "Jones'."

Then there are the lies we tell others, usually because we don't want to tell the truth.

"The check is in the mail."

"I'll get right on it."

"Let's catch up soon."

You might argue that these are all part of our social contract. All part of the etiquette we use to lubricate interactions. After all, I'm just being "polite."

Well, what would happen if you stopped being polite and started connecting with the truth?

I don't mean run out in the street and tell everyone you think they're a fat cow and you don't ever want to speak to them again.

I mean, figure out who you DO want to connect with, spend time with and include in your inner circle. What would happen if you acted on that truth?

Instead of fake niceties, what would happen if you surrounded yourself with the people you love? Even if they're far away, it's easier than ever to make contact.

Modern technology allows you to connect instantly, anywhere, anytime. You could use your phone, Facetime, Skype, Zoom, email, and many other electronic miracles. You could even use snail mail.

The worst of all are the lies we tell ourselves.

I'm not good enough.

I'll do it tomorrow.

I can't.

These do the most damage. I don't know of a single human who hasn't buried themselves in such untruth on a regular basis. It's true whether you admit it or not, or whether you are aware of it or not.

These lies, or stories, we tell ourselves repeatedly about who we are, and what we can and can't do, are all made up.

Why do I choose to believe I can't? Why do I choose to believe I can?

Henry Ford was right when he said, "There are those who believe they can and those who believe they can't, and they're both right."

What do you choose to believe right now?

Which stories about you or your life would you like to change?

Which stories are no longer serving your highest good?

Is there a story you'd rather tell about yourself and your life from this moment on?

It is likely that up until now you accepted and believed all the stories people told you. Now you know, you can investigate and decide which ones work and disregard the rest.

You will be the author of your own new story. If you don't create your own, which one would you prefer?

These questions will help you eliminate chaos in your life and get focused on what you want, not what someone else told you, or what you think you wanted yesterday.

CHAPTER 31

What is the Meaning Behind That?

I grew up with a pack of wolves. Not in the "Dances With Wolves" sense, but I was the only girl with six brothers. We were close in age, and we were treated like one giant "pack."

My eldest brother was three and a half years old when I was born, and I was child number four, three more followed right after me.

It's funny how children who grow up in big families often attach a number to their identity. Brother #6 uses his number in one of his email accounts to this day. My Skype address has my "number" in it longue4.

I think that because I was the only girl, I wanted to be special. My grandparents showered attention on me. Both of my grandmothers spent extra time with me, and I truly did feel special.

At home, I was supposed to fit in and be one of the "pack" because there were too many of us, and there just wasn't any way to get my parents attention.

From my brothers' viewpoint, I was a spoiled brat who had my own room. I was the only girl, and they all had to share a room with one or more brothers. I was okay with that.

My parents' story is that they were very busy. Since I was the "good" one, they didn't need to watch me as closely as my brothers. To me, it felt like being ignored.

Maybe they felt that way because the police never came to the door to ask for me. Because that happened with some of the boys, it became our inside joke.

I did indeed want to please my parents and be "good," but what I have learned is that our memories are so fickle that I'm not even sure many things I think I remember actually happened.

The relevant point here is that we can learn a great truth when we notice how differently we all apply meaning to the same event.

Who's right?

If my version of the "truth" is right, is everyone else wrong?

NO clearly not. If I ask myself what is "true"? What is real? I can begin to sort out my reality.

The answer can be any story I choose. I'm not talking about pretending here. I am talking about closely examining the truth behind the meaning we attach to events in our lives.

Today I have freed myself by noticing that much of what I believe is all just a story I made up in my head.

I can choose to review and acknowledge all the other stories that coexist at the same time.

It suddenly puts everything into a very different perspective.

The writings of Dr. Helen Schucman and her iconic *A Course in Miracles* takes everyone through the exercise of removing all meaning from the objects we attach meaning to especially the stories from our past.

I shared August birthdays with some of the "boys" from the time they were born. Both Mike and Jim and I were all born in August. Because our birthdays are so close together, we were the proverbial "Irish twins."

Starting when I was about 10, I no longer got a birthday on my birthday. We had a group cake on some random day in August when everyone could get together. In hindsight, I was not okay with that. The advantage is that I feel like I can celebrate my birthday on any day, the disadvantage is that I don't take any actual birthday very seriously, and many people I know are fanatical about celebrating on their "special day."

This added fuel to the story that I wasn't really special. I didn't even deserve my own birthday. Especially in my teens, I began to see many events through the eyes of that same story.

When the shared birthday tradition began, I didn't feel left out at all. At some point along the way, I added a new meaning. It was just one more piece of evidence that pointed to a truth I had now come to accept. That somehow, I wasn't significant.

With seven children in 13 ½ years, I know my mom didn't attach any unusual significance to the combined birthdays. I'm sure it was a pragmatic choice. Let's just have one big party in August. I can cook one big cake and clean up one mess instead of having three cakes, three parties, and three messes.

I imagine it was probably just a question of survival.

As the years went on, I've learned another way to look at the situation. What if the story is that I have three birthdays in August and I get to celebrate any of them or all of them?

I now celebrate my birthday for the entire month of August. I have a million birthdays. I must be really special. Moreover, I also create meaningful events around that story.

I'm sure that people born around Christmas might feel the same. Parents get busy, days go by and then the inevitable, "why don't we get you one big present for Christmas and your birthday instead of celebrating two things?"

How we felt about that at the time, as adults, we can choose to remember these stories without any emotional charge if we choose to review it from a different perspective.

My story about not being special, because I was "part of the pack," was a story that hindered me for a long time. It may sound crazy because I am certain that's not what my parents intended.

One effect this story had on me was that I became ultra-competitive in my attempt to get noticed by my parents. This showed up in many ways at various times in my youth. This was perceived as a "masculine" trait. This was not good.

After all, girls in Catholic schools weren't supposed to compete. Eventually, this stigma won out. So, I turned back into a wallflower and tried not to be noticed.

We even attach meaning to something as simple as rain.

So, what is the meaning of rain?

If you're inside reading a book, the rain probably has very little to with anything, and we probably don't attach meaning at all.

On the other hand, if you're getting married, you might worry that the rain will ruin the festivities in some way. Or you might decide that God doesn't like you because it's raining on your wedding day.

If you're a farmer or living in an area of drought, you might openly welcome rain to help the soil, grow your crops, and fill the reservoirs.

The feelings and beliefs we have ALL come from the meaning WE attach to events. Words, tone, expression, frame of mind, and a hundred other things all interplay to create this meaning.

We are not given these beliefs; we make them up as we go.

We invent our own meanings for the events in our life. We take these meanings and turn them into bedrock truth. Then they become stuck in our heads, hearts, and bodies, seemingly unchangeable.

What if we could replace our current meaning with a completely different meaning for some event in our lives? Especially those critical events and beliefs that come from our childhood experience.

We see that these experiences are powerful and seem to establish our core beliefs and values, which in turn affect all our interactions as adults.

What if it was possible to eliminate the negative charge attached to past events that hold bad meaning for us? What if we, in effect, could rewrite the story so that we can see, and come to accept, a completely different meaning associated with a particular event?

We see that possibility dramatically unfold when a person rises to great heights following a traumatic event or personal tragedy. At the same time, we see a different person with a similar tragedy fall miserably into a heap.

We are all inspired by the ability of the first group to overcome challenges, and the other group you never hear about. These people never get over it but stay mired in thought, fear, and tragedy for the rest of their lives.

Does it surprise you to realise that you can choose what meaning you attach to events?

Does it surprise you to learn that you can choose what story you tell yourself about every event or person in your life?

Is it encouraging to learn that all this is in your control and can shape your peace and happiness starting today?

"What if, instead of justifying your anger, you looked deep inside yourself for the internal causes that may be operating?"

– Barbara Longue

CHAPTER 32

It's An Inside Job

Have you ever had a conversation with a colleague or loved one where it's all going just fine until they say that one thing, one <u>little</u> thing, and you fly off the handle in rage or anger?

Did you ever notice that when you're in the middle of a major destructive emotion, like anger or frustration, you often blame everything and everyone else for being wrong or having wronged you? Why did they say that? Why did they do that? What's wrong with them?

Sound familiar?

Our closest colleagues and loved ones often know our triggers better than we do. They certainly know how to exploit them, don't they? Perhaps we do the same.

How easily are we offended when someone says something that we choose to interpret as an insult, even knowing that it may not have been intended that way at all?

With anger, for example, I'm sure you can think of many situations that easily trigger you. The most challenging aspect of that truth is that the better someone knows us, the easier it is for them to trigger us.

So, as nice as it is to believe it, is it entirely their fault that they're setting off these little time bombs in our head? Or, is it something that we do to ourselves?

Fortunately, for all of us, it really is an INSIDE job, and the cause of the emotion is not the external influence.

Did the constructive criticism trigger a childhood emotion of not being good enough? Or, hearing from our parents that "you will never make it"? Maybe it stemmed from some other nonsense that lives deep within our subconscious.

Are those incidents caused by "other people?" Is the onus on them for saying certain things? Or, are we responsible for knowing our triggers that come from old defense mechanisms and old thinking?

Maybe, just maybe, we can recognize that truth that allows us to take control and release the underlying and automatic reaction.

What if we accept responsibility for knowing ourselves well enough to identify the ticking time bombs that can be triggered this way?

What if we accept responsibility for knowing that we can attach a different meaning, not just to the current event that triggered our anger, but to the underlying deep anger we've been clutching? This is anger that came from someone else or some different circumstance.

What if we accept the fact that the anger and resentment might not be about an external person or thing at all, but recognized that it's an inside job created in our own thinking?

What if, instead of justifying your anger, you looked deep inside yourself for the internal causes that may be operating?

What if, instead of seeking retaliation or revenge, you asked yourself if what you believe is true? What if you asked about your role in the incident? What if you were open to accepting some responsibility for the bad feelings?

For decades, we have been trying to become more empathic and more understanding of people's feelings and emotions.

Today, it seems that many of us have created a brand-new problem by becoming oversensitive to relatively minor situations. It hurts when others don't know how to deal effectively with our viewpoints and feelings.

What if it was possible to speak with those around you in a way that was not insulting or offensive?

I believe that the world has become enormously sensitive and empathic. (Except the current sitting U.S. president and the people who voted for him.)

This ultra-sensitivity to the feelings and emotions of others can be pushed to the extreme. Those who experience such sensitivity are called empaths.

Here is one definition of an empath: a person who makes psychological identification with others, or experiences vicarious feelings, thoughts or attitudes of another.

Until they learn how to separate what feelings and emotions are their own from the feelings and emotions of others, life can be a living hell.

The good news is that such awareness and control is possible. You may think this is crazy, but it's true.

I was a "raging empath" until I learned to control my thoughts and feelings using internal or spiritual martial arts.

My first class in the internal martial art of psychic self-defense was held in the SoHo section of Manhattan. The old loft was located on a corner, and it felt like I needed some kind of self-defense just to walk to the building.

It was my first experience understanding how to dissect and separate the thoughts that were mine, and mine alone, and the thoughts and doubts other people were inserting into my consciousness.

The process was based on ancient Taoist meditation techniques to control one's mind for self-protection.

This was the first time I realized how much I had been picking up on portions of other people's thoughts and interpreting them in my own unhelpful, and even, warped way.

It was a double whammy. First, I was picking up on other people's thoughts, and second, I went on to misinterpret them, or attach a negative meaning to them that didn't exist.

One of the biggest challenges for people experiencing stress and anxiety is the inability to know what thoughts and feelings are their own, and separating those from thoughts and feelings which belong to others, to which they may be reacting in an empathetic fashion.

I learned a simple clearing technique in my martial arts training that is unceremoniously called the "dumping" exercise. I highly recommend that everyone do this every day. It's amazing what crap we pick up during the day and how easy it is to get rid of it. For videos on how to do this, visit our website at www.vortexhealingcentre.com.

CHAPTER 33

Mindfulness

Mindfulness is one of the biggest buzzwords floating around right now. Why is that so?

According to Tim Ferriss, 80% of the billionaires, icons, and world-class performers on the planet today have some type of mindfulness practice in their daily routines.

So think about this. If top performers across every industry are practicing some type of mindfulness, why would anyone dismiss this practice as some kind of a new age, hippy thing? What do these people know that the average Joe doesn't?

Some people begin the practice of mindfulness to relieve stress. According to Headspace, their panic button usage rose 300% shortly after Trump's election.

Others come to the practice to increase focus and to train the mind.

Still others are beginning a mindfulness practice to relieve physical and emotional symptoms like heart conditions and depression.

I'm not pretending I'm perfect in this practice. I haven't always done it daily, but every single time it is part of my daily routine, I experience great inner peace and an ability to achieve whatever goals I set.

There are many forms of mindfulness practice. The simplest is being aware of the breath. Take ONE conscious breath.

Conscious, meaning directing each thought to the experience of breathing.

Can you commit to taking just ONE conscious breath in your day? It forces you to bring your attention from wherever it is to right here, right now.

It's impossible to not be "in the present" when you're breathing consciously. It returns you to the moment. It leaves all your worries and fears about the past in the past and obliges you to drop all future worries and fears.

It's impossible to be present with the breath and be somewhere else. Moreover, that one moment away from all distractions, worries, and fears begins healing the mental, physical, emotional, and spiritual bodies.

It takes a bit of practice to train the mind to focus on the breath, and this mind training is what mindfulness is all about. You're learning how to take back control of your thoughts, your breath, and your experience as a human being.

I meet many people who think they are terrible at meditation, or that it's just too hard. I always try to help them understand that it's called "mindfulness practice" because we are practicing.

It's like practicing anything else; repetition is key. As time passes, it becomes easier to sense how your own body and mind work.

I create my daily ritual so that my mindfulness practice is in the morning, sometimes even before I've gotten out of bed. I use it to set my day exactly the way I would like it to play out.

When I miss mindfulness practice in the morning, I feel something's missing throughout the day. That makes me eager to get back to that place of quiet breathing, of conscious breath.

For the last few months, I've been recording many mini-mindfulness sessions. Most are 1 to 3 minutes long, so they are easy to follow. You can find them using the link below.

https://www.youtube.com/vortexhealingcentreinctas

I encourage you to create space in your life where you owe nothing to anyone else; this is all for you.

One of my favorite authors on the topic is Chade-Meng Tan, Google employee #107. He helps giant companies like Google keep their employees sane, even in the most intense work environment.

Here are some of his tips on how to create a Mindfulness practice.

How to Create and Sustain a Mindfulness Practice

1. Have a Buddy

Have a "mindfulness" buddy and commit to chatting every week about how your practice is going.

End the conversation with, "How did this conversation go?" (being mindful of our conversation)

If you subscribe to our YouTube channel, you can ask questions. You can also make comments on our Facebook page at www.facebook.com/vortexhealingcentre7215.

2. Do Less Than You Can

For highly productive people, this may seem like a cop-out. However, it is effective and powerful. The idea is to do less than you are capable of so that your mindfulness practice never feels like a burden or a chore.

You want to keep the practice from becoming tiresome.

Sit often for short periods, and your mindfulness practice will develop into a luxury that draws you to it regularly.

3. Take One Mindful Breath Each Day

Just one mindful breath each day is your first commitment. Once that's done, everything else is a bonus.

Notice how your breath feels when you're in the middle of it. Notice how it feels when you're consumed by other things.

Feel free to add bonus breaths/minutes. Always do LESS than you think you can do.

Some great books to learn more:

Chade-Meng Tan's *Search Inside Yourself* and *Joy On Demand* is one of the most practical books on meditation.

Jon Kabat-Zinn *Wherever You Go, There You Are*

Dalai Lama – Any book he's written.

"You can't be angry and grateful simultaneously. You can't be fearful and grateful simultaneously. Gratitude is the antidote to the things that mess us up."

~ Tony Robbins

CHAPTER 34

Gratitude Porn

My advice is to become a raving lunatic about being grateful. Do it so often people will think you're obsessed and crazy.

I saw the phrase "gratitude porn" used in a negative sense like it's possible to have too much gratitude. Whoever said that doesn't know how it works.

I don't think we can ever have enough gratitude. Gratitude for simple things like who we are and the gifts we're given.

Most people are familiar with the concept of repeatedly writing a list of things that you are grateful for, but if that's all you do it's easy to get stuck expressing your gratitude for the same things again and again.

The truth is that you can't be too grateful too often. It is entirely appropriate to be grateful for the same things, over and over. Repetition creates a deeper and deeper connection with the objects of gratitude.

I make expressing gratitude part of my morning thoughts and meditation before I get out of bed each morning – first up is a real expression of gratitude for simply being alive.

Again.

Then I add being grateful for something specific that happened the previous day. Then I add something specific about someone I care about, perhaps someone in my family or among my friends.

Then, and especially, I add being grateful for the chance to experience life again this present day. Life with all the infinite possibilities the day might hold – all the magic, mystery, and miracles that might be right around the corner.

When you start your day off like that, it's hard not to begin noticing more magic, mysteries, and miracles occurring all around you.

Life is magic.

Life is an adventure.

It's up to you to call it forth.

Bring it to the forefront of your mind.

Only then start your day.

At this moment, I am so grateful that I live at a time of such momentous beauty and change in the world. We all have the opportunity to sculpt each day and the world we experience.

Some people think that being grateful means being "satisfied" or "settling" for less than you can be. That somehow, if you're too grateful, you won't be able to achieve greater heights.

This misguided view comes from the notion that only dissatisfaction creates momentum for change. In fact, it is gratitude that can most powerfully help you get out of bed when you're struggling through depression.

Gratitude can help you connect to just how much you love and appreciate your family and friends. It's gratitude that can help you appreciate your best talents so that you can stay focused on what you do well so that you can do more of it.

It's gratitude that can help you surrender to the fact that you don't need to always "be the best" at everything you set out to do. This creates the freedom to focus on what you do well and have the greatest joy in that.

We based self-improvement myths of the past on the premise that somehow, you were not okay as you are and that you needed "improving." I bought into that myth fully.

The truth is that you don't need any "improving." You are perfect just the way you are. What needs some attention is your ability to appreciate your existence and experiences just as they happened.

You can be profoundly grateful for the simple fact that you are here to experience your human existence, including all of the perceived frailties and faults.

Perhaps, it's these very "limitations" that make you truly unique, that make you who you are. It is these "limitations" that you should be most grateful for.

They are a gift to help you become your own hero as you make choices to experience growth. This growth comes as we eliminate frailties, faults, and limitations and experience a true connection to joy, love, and happiness.

This is your journey.

Make the most of it.

Here are some ways I've tried adding more gratitude in my own life.

Calendar Reminder Every Day

I set my phone reminder for 1:00 p.m. Why, 1:00 p.m.? It doesn't matter what time. 1:00 p.m. is just the moment in my day when I'm starting to get a bit tired. That brief moment of gratitude gets me over the hump to have a great second half of my day.

Create A Gratitude Journal

I like handwriting these thoughts. Research has demonstrated that writing stimulates the brain in different ways than just thinking, speaking or entering things in a computer.

As life unfolds, more often than not, I notice that I have left my journal somewhere else at the very moment I feel particularly inspired to write something down.

As a substitute, I use the note-taking function on my phone or "Google Keep," so I don't forget things.

Looking back on what I've written is a great way to help me out of a slump, whether the slump is mental, physical, emotional, or spiritual. It reminds me of the feelings of gratitude and connection that I've already experienced.

Gratitude Meditation

I add a brief gratitude moment in my meditation practice while I'm still lying in bed before I get up to start my day. I find this one thing to be a source of amazing feelings of happiness and satisfaction in my life. It also instantly stops any negative thoughts that want to creep in.

Celebrate Thanksgiving Every Day

How many ways can you add the words "Thank You" into your daily life at work or home?

Isn't that the true meaning of Thanksgiving? Giving Thanks?

So often during our day, we feel inclined to offer a long explanation when a simple "thank you" would be the model of powerful and elegant simplicity.

CHAPTER 35

Time Abundance

Here is a little quiz to set the stage for thinking about how we use or abuse the time we have.

How often do you experience some kind of struggle related to:

Thinking there's not enough time?
- Thinking about work when at home?
- Thinking about home when at work?
- Thinking you can't do what you want because you don't have time?
- Being bored with too much time so you try "killing time?"

What if the truth is that you have all the time you want?

Often, we don't realise how much our thinking is related to time, especially the belief that there is a shortage of time in both your work and personal aspects of your life.

Einstein's mathematics and experiments with relativity conclusively demonstrate that time is not fixed. It is flexible, depending on the velocity of your travel.

The flexibility extends beyond the measurement of elapsed seconds on a moving timepiece in an experiment. There is also perceptual flexibility that occurs in our minds.

Did you ever have the feeling when a second lasted like almost forever? It might have been when you were proposed to by your fiancée when every moment was magic as you gazed deeply into each other's eyes.

It may have been during a car accident when you saw everything coming like slow motion and watched it happen like a movie. Even after the fact, the movie may still play exactly that way in your mind.

How about those occasions when time speeds up without your awareness? Maybe you got home after a long drive and have no idea what happened on the way. You were on autopilot and not noticing much of anything.

Time is like that. It is as flexible as you would like it to be.

The challenge is to bend time in the way YOU would like it.

Here are some easy ways to practice shifting your mindset to bend time.

Mind Shift # 1 – Eliminate Time Scarcity and Overwhelm

The first step is learning to differentiate between the urgent and the important.

If you find yourself regularly saying things like: "I don't have enough time, or, "There is not enough time," you are a victim of this affliction.

Step one is to stop using time as an excuse. Get clear about the truth, which is really: "I don't want to do this," or, "I have other priorities right now that are more important to me."

Step two is to start realizing that "being busy" is an excuse. You start believing the lie that there is not enough time.

It's common these days when someone asks how you're doing to say, "Busy as ever." What does that even mean?

It is as if being busy is somehow a suitable replacement for doing what you love, being happy, finding joy in your daily life and many other things.

There is another part to this that shows up as a belief, "if I don't 'do everything,' something bad will happen." That bad thing often remains unspecified, but it seems powerful.

So, how do you eliminate this belief?

One way is to end the practice of simply rolling over uncompleted tasks from one day's to-do list, to the next day. You may believe the myth that you must complete all of those tasks. The truth is that you don't.

Your mind may scream at you: "Yeah, but I have to do all those things." Simply getting into that idea is a cop-out. Maybe it's true, but maybe it's not.

Since we all know that we do our best work when we're centered and focused, a more powerful, truthful and productive belief is, "I have all the time in the world."

If you begin each day and each hour with that truth firmly centered in your consciousness, and you proceed by doing just one thing at a time fully and completely, you will get more done and be happier.

Mind Shift # 2 – Develop Patient Timelines

Create a larger buffer zone around all projects by including travel time, interruption time, delay time, and time for setbacks.

You may be inclined to say that it is a waste of time. The truth is the opposite.

Most things take MUCH longer than we anticipate. When you give yourself way more time than you think you need, you eliminate the pressure of scarcity and the negative impact stress has on your productivity and creativity.

That saves time and allows you to complete tasks better and faster. Then, when you are ahead of schedule, with the job done right the first time, all the extra time you have is a bonus.

Setting patient timelines eliminates an enormous source of stress we passively live with most of the time. This stress has real consequences in terms of project completion, and in terms of our physical and mental health.

Another tool to increase efficiency, satisfaction, and productivity, and therefore increase your available time, is to set smaller goals and clear near-term deadlines.

Choosing to set smaller and more achievable goals creates more "wins," this allows more dopamine in the brain and leads to a sense of satisfaction. This chemical not only feels good but also creates more efficient action and higher enjoyment.

This doesn't mean to give yourself all the time in the world to get everything done. That is not efficiency or creating time. That is laziness or a manifestation that you don't want to do it.

For example, if you decide you want to write a book, you might think that setting a patient timeline would be giving yourself a year to finish the project.

That may or may not be true. It may take a year to write the book, but if you don't set aside time consistently to write you will find yourself scrambling at the last hour to write your book in a weekend.

That's how I wrote many of my college papers and I realise now how much self-imposed stress I added to my life.

Breaking down your big project into tiny projects that are achievable and trackable is the fastest way to create time abundance.

I've had writer's block every time I thought of sitting down to write. It seemed like a permanent problem. To create a win, I created a schedule where I do a 40-minute session within an hour of waking up.

During that time, I write something, anything. It might be journaling for a thousand words or it might be working on this manuscript, but it will be something.

When I've finished that block, I can declare myself finished for the day, or keep going. That's how you expand time, by doing something that you say you're going do — creating completion by the commitment and then action.

Mind Shift # 3 – Master Boredom

Another terrifying phrase in our society is "killing time." Why on earth would we want to waste the only irreplaceable resource?

Why do we create numbness by immediately jumping straight into Facebook, some other social media, television, or email?

Instead, choose to do nothing. Be fully present to this exact moment and notice what's happening right around you. Take this moment to appreciate where you are right now.

Because I live so far from anywhere, I get to practice this often on my ridiculously long flights. I used to think the 6-8 hour flights from New York to Paris were long. Those are a pleasant memory.

Now I'm routinely on a plane for 14-15 hours per segment, with travel time extending 22-33 hours. Learning how to make mindfulness moments is part of what keeps me sane.

I use a playlist of meditations. I have a routine set of exercises. I have designated writing time and topics. Also, I have a list of specific tasks that show up over and over again around the property.

All these tools, combined with an active choice to be fully present to whatever I pick to do, increase my productivity, help me maintain my sanity, and create time.

Mastering boredom means learning how to sit quietly with your thoughts and feelings, without depending on the buzz from a phone, television or email to stimulate you.

Becoming good at mastering your mind is the fastest way to eliminate boredom and the need to "kill" time.

CHAPTER 36

Choose Yourself First

When I talk to people about choosing themselves first, the conversation invariably turns to the topic of "selfishness." Choosing yourselfrealise first is not selfishness.

Choosing yourself first is about learning how to add things to your day that are for you and focused entirely on you. This choice is not in the context of selfishness, but in the context of making yourself the most powerful person, you can be.

As parents and employees in a company, we do things for everyone else all the time. We're constantly rushing around trying to please our boss, our spouse, our kids, our teachers, and our neighbors.

When do we set aside time to do what WE want to do? If you don't create time intentionally, then the answer will be "never."

When I was a busy working parent raising two children, I found it a real struggle to fit in a one-hour yoga class each Saturday morning.

It only happened if I woke up on time, nothing else got in the way, and I could escape from the house without being sidetracked.

If that didn't happen, I missed it, and nothing else in the schedule made up for it. That was it. That ME time was probably gone for the week.

I found myself rushing from one event to another, racing up and down the highway picking the kids up, dropping them off and wondering at the end of the day where my day went.

As I have visited with many people, I know this is a common story. So, how do we make a significant and immediate change?

There are a million ways to start practicing putting yourself first.

One of the easiest ways is to start showing kindness and compassion for yourself. Stop beating yourself up for what you did or didn't do.

Another quick and simple way that takes no time and costs nothing is to practice showing appreciation to yourself for things you have done well.

What this looks like will differ for each person. The essence is simply to recognise that if you don't take care of your own body, spirit, and heart, you will not be in a place of power to care effectively for those people and things most important to you.

The purpose of this chapter is to have you consider how you can choose yourself first — no more waiting for someone else to acknowledge you. I want YOU to acknowledge YOU.

Right now, write down ten things you've done well. After you write down the thing you did well, write out the exact language of praise and appreciation, you would love most to hear.

Then, give that list to yourself and read it out loud slowly and joyfully. Do it with enthusiasm. Cut yourself some slack. Ready, Set, Go!

If you can't find ten things, stop lying to yourself. You know right this minute there are many more than ten things if you are fair about yourself. Even if you have to include a few things you wish you had done, include them.

Have fun. Make this joyful. Don't stop. Just keep writing.

1. _____

_____

_____

2. _____

_____

_____

3. _____

_____

_____

4. _____

_____

_____

5.

6.

7.

8.

9.

10.

In case you struggle writing something to describe what a great job you did, here are some examples:

Job Well Done!

- You did a damn good job handling that emergency last week. I'm really glad you were here to take care of it.
- You know, I don't say thank you very often, but I want you to know that I appreciate everything you do to help make my job easier.
- I don't know what we would do without you. That was good work!

The best part about choosing yourself first is that you will be able to immediately notice anywhere you feel resentment or anger because this praise didn't come from another person.

One trap to avoid is the feeling of frustration if the exercise above seems difficult.

If you find the exercise difficult and you feel resentments coming up as you do it, then write all those resentments down on a piece of paper. Getting those resentments out of your head is critical for learning to choose yourself first.

It is way past time to get all of that nonsense and harmful energy out of your head and your heart. Throw it down on paper for now. Don't treat anything as "too small." If it brings up feelings of resentment, write it down.

CHAPTER 37

Create Your Day

Another amazing tool available with just a little effort is learning to "create your day."

Since 80% of most successful people create and practice a morning routine to kickstart their day, it is absolutely worth learning what these seemingly "super people" do to accomplish so much more than mere mortals.

Taken back to basics, such a routine creates new habits to start your day with simple practices that enhance the main aspects of your life.

Not someone else's life.

Not what someone else wants you to do.

This is your life, your gifts, your power, and your ritual. Doing this allows you to establish a deep connection to yourself, your family, friends, and other aspects of life critical to you.

For example, I do something that acknowledges and strengthens each of the following life areas of my life every morning before I go to "work," whatever it may be for that day.

1. Mental

2. Physical

3. Emotional

4. Spiritual

5. Project (important but not urgent)

I think of it as strengthening each of the "bodies" that make up our existence.

By choosing every day to focus even a small amount of attention on moving in the direction I want in each life area, I find that I continually make progress on my goals and stay balanced in this crazy world.

You know how easy it is to get sidetracked with electronic devices, or with making a living and breathing, distractions that are all around us.

Spouses, children, friends, social media, and all the other aspects of daily life keep us continually "busy." Being busy or distracted or overwhelmed is easy. Everybody is doing it.

What most people don't know is how quickly they can come back into focus on what they truly want to experience in life. The fastest and simplest way to create the life I want is to focus on creating it one day at a time.

You've certainly heard all the motivational quotes like: "A journey of a thousand miles begins with a single step." Or, the joke that still makes me laugh, "How do you eat an elephant? One bite at a time."

They're all designed to remind us we don't actually take quantum leaps. Rather, life is a series of tiny steps in the right direction that we make happen every single day.

When we have those inevitable days that don't flow as we wish, we have to start over, even if it's mid-day.

The challenge of creating a new morning habit can seem very daunting for many people.

Realizing how many top performers have regular routines that keep them centered and give them power was a motivating drive that helped me begin to accomplish what I wanted.

However, you can't do it all at once. You have to do it and do it and do it until it becomes a habit. That's when the magic kicks in.

When you can consistently move forward in the direction you'd like to go, even a little bit at a time, everything starts to move.

For some reason, all of us constantly overestimate what we can do in one day. It is also true that we wildly underestimate what we can accomplish in one year with consistent action.

In addition to learning what actions to take, it is just as important, in many cases, to learn what NOT to do.

Learning to say no. Learning how to stop. Remembering what silence is. Remembering to simply BE, and that just being is enough.

Remembering to connect to the true source of infinite power and wisdom, which lives in every one of us.

Believe me; it's impossible to maintain a higher state of consciousness and play on Facebook at the same time. I've tried it. It's just not possible.

Here are some ideas and best practices to create your day:

Research and learn the routines that highly successful people do every day to maintain their health and sanity. Which of those practices would help you?

For example, a recent informal survey by Tim Ferriss, from his podcast guests, showed 80% of billionaires meditate every day. Imagine, those who make the most money spend "empty time" in silent meditation.

One simple way to create a new daily routine is to start with just a 15-minute segment. Get up 15 minutes earlier. Use that 15 minutes specifically for your personal care ritual.

In 15 minutes, you could do a 3-minute mini mindfulness routine and then add a 4-minute high-intensity exercise circuit. You could then rest and focus for 3 minutes.

Or, you could sit for the entire time with your favorite person and a cup of hot coffee, without reading the paper or doing anything else and just enjoying the space together.

For those who have asked me about the ritual I create for self-care, I have broken down my ritual into five areas, as follows:

Mental: 10 Ideas. Have some fun, write them down and make no judgements. This is an amazing way to increase mental power and creativity.

Physical: Exercise. 7-minute workout, Sun Salutation, Walk the Dogs, Qi Gong.

Emotional: Connecting. I call, email, or text my kids or mother with special notes or pictures about where I am or what I'm doing.

Spiritual: Meditation. In 3 minutes or less, imagine what your perfect day would look like if somehow everything miraculously flows smoothly. What experience would you like to have?

Business Project: 20-minute segment on a project that's not urgent, but very important

This might not seem significant, but I can promise you that with the accumulated effort, it makes a huge difference. Rather than think about things in gigantic chunks, what is the smallest possible step to do something for yourself to make your day start and finish great?

The short morning exercise segment is one of the most important parts of this ritual, and one that is most frequently neglected.

This might happen because you're going to "work out" later by playing some sport or going to the gym. Nothing prevents you from doing that in addition to the brief exercise in your morning routine.

More often than not, exercise scheduled later in the day doesn't happen, or if it does, it turns out to be a halfhearted attempt at some cardio or something similar while the mind is distracted, and the energy is elsewhere.

Since exercise is one of the most engaging and empowering things to connect your mind and your body, sharpen your focus and get your internal engine firing on all cylinders, neglecting this is fatal.

Short exercise segments do not mean sloppy exercise segments. Making this short exercise a period of high-intensity activity is a way to keep it easy, short, simple, and powerful.

On top of that, scientific research demonstrates that small, very intense bursts of activity create a significant heart-healthy impact.

Many popular, high intensity, short duration exercise programs available are both effective and fun, including the Japanese Tabata.

My experience with hundreds of clients demonstrates that if we don't exercise, we're even more tired at the end of the day and we still can't sleep.

Also critical to this practice is learning to stop and breathe. The 3-minute mini mindfulness practice is one of the easiest and simplest ways to learn how to stop, let go and remember the infinite power and wisdom that we all contain.

Each aspect of the 5-part system is essential. Some of them you may already do very well, so adding the others will be a snap.

Some aspects you may have neglected for long periods, getting that going might require some effort.

It's amazing what happens when you actively take care of the "five bodies" before you kick off the rest of your day.

For me, it has helped me stay connected to my family and myself while completing a massive and life-changing move and career change. At the same time, have the energy and stability to do it without losing my mind.

"What life-changing things would you like to see in your life?"

"What is the first tiny step you can take in that direction today?"

— Barbara Longue

CHAPTER 38

Awakened Profitability Coaching

As you've read through this book, you saw how my life was defined by my recent awakening and all of the many ways I was able to change my relationship with money, family, and happiness to achieve the life that I want. Now I can help you achieve those same goals.

They apply very specifically to business in the same way they apply to your personal life. Figuring out what your big vision is for your business is the same process as figuring out what your big vision is for your life.

How you live your day is how successful your business will be.

If you're constantly running around or distracted by every bright shiny object, there's no way you're hitting your business targets.

Achieving your business targets and creating cash flow is the easiest way to create more adventures for yourself in your personal life. Eliminating the money and cash flow problem is the best way to start creating that confidence in yourself. Paradoxically, it's even to create more money and more success once you eliminate many of the fears and daily habits that no longer serve your highest good and replace them with new habits that fit your goals and your deepest desires.

The question is, will you continue doing the same things you're currently doing, or are you willing to take a step forward and create momentum. The time is now, and you can feel it to the core of your being.

This is why I would like to personally invite you to step up and say:

"Count me in.

I want to make a difference.

I want to Wake Up and Create the Business and Life of My Dreams."

Go to www.globetrottingentrepreneur.com to discover how to be clear on what direction you should take in your business and in your life, strategies for moving forward, and ideas on how to maximise your profits and minimise your efforts.

Afterword

I write this after a nine-month hiatus following a traumatic brain injury.

Just one month after meeting with JT Foxx and determining that the best title for this book should be Money, Family, Sex and Happiness: You Can Have It All, I fell while on a walk with the horse and hit my head on a rock and suffered a traumatic brain injury. While I didn't need an operation, the brain bleed, and three days in the hospital made me question even more deeply once again, what is the meaning behind our existence.

For the first eight weeks, I couldn't do much of anything but a little gardening and a short walk around the property.

Then another eight weeks to be able to sit in a car and leave my beautiful spot on the hill nestled in the forest overlooking the ocean without getting nauseous and suffering more massive headaches.

It's taken this long to get enough brain power to be able to sit at my laptop and return to this manuscript and figure out what I wanted to say.

Reading through the manuscript has been quite cathartic, and I have had to remind myself of the habits I need to return to as part of my healing process.

I, too, have had to start all over yet again.

My consciousness for the first few months lived in a massive quantum universe so immense and profound and filled with the purest form of love and light that I found it hard to return to my human body that was surrounded by pain, dizziness and massive headaches, difficulty walking and even remembering to feed myself.

It's been an amazing experience to be able to share my story with others who will hopefully be inspired to take action themselves to live life to the fullest every moment. To find what is truly important to you.

The title of the book is the tagline to reel you in so that you can get to the deeper questions of how to determine what brings deep meaning and satisfaction in your business and your life so you too can create a space where happiness lives. For most entrepreneurs, your business is your life and creating a space that is congruent with your true values of what is important to you not what you think should be important to you or what you've been told to believe should be important to you.

It's made me even more committed to training others to generate passive streams of income so that they can get down to the business of living a full life. If your business is consuming all of your free time and making you feel stressed and out of sorts, I can help you to grow your business quickly so that you can hire the help you need and make sure you have passive income so that you can work or not work as YOU choose.

When you get your business in order, it's much easier to get your life in order.

You can stop being the biggest block to your success by creating your habits and meaningful desires.

For most people, it's easier for me to help them generate or turnaround their business and seeing where this time-starved life can find deeper meaning and fulfillment once they've taken care of their mental, physical, emotional and spiritual needs. Not what someone else says they need, but what they are craving deep inside that brings them a deep connection to their soul.

Appendix and Contact Information

For access to the resources I've talked about in this book, you can find them at the following sites:

My website: www.barbaralongue.com,

The Vortex Healing Centre at www.vortexhealingcentre.com

YouTube: www.youtube.com/vortexhealingcentreinctas where you'll find nearly 200 mini mindfulness moments.

Facebook: https://www.facebook.com/barbaralongue

Instagram: https://www.instagram.com/blongue

Business Test: http://bit.ly/BizQuizLE

Please feel free to email me at barbara@barbaralongue.com

Acknowledgments

This has been an amazing journey to find my voice. I had the support of so many people who provided their talent and personal encouragement to help me complete this book.

My deepest appreciation goes out to each of them.

I am grateful to my amazing editor and coach, Kellan Fluckiger. Thanks for all of your help over the past few years.

Deep gratitude to JT Foxx and Coach Cherie Eilertson for their assistance in helping me to move forward.

I want to thank Kaylen Jorgensen professionalism, enthusiasm, and proofreading skills were a great benefit to me.

I especially want to thank Sue for her patience and understanding as this project evolved.

Of course, I want to thanks all of the entrepreneurs and business owners I've worked with over the years who have inspired me in so many ways.

About the Author

Barbara Longue is an entrepreneur, speaker, cryptocurrency investor, business rebound strategist and co-founder of the Vortex Healing Centre, mindfulness, coaching, and training centre.

The Centre helps both start-up and seasoned business owners achieve their higher purpose and create higher profits and a better work environment for themselves and their employees. She is a speaker on entrepreneurial success, creating a passive income, and wildly growing your profitability.

As Co-Founder of the Vortex Healing Centre, a non-profit, Barbara oversees the development of new products and services to help the next generation of conscious global leaders raise their awareness and find deeper meaning in their day to day business.

Barbara has been influenced by martial arts and both Eastern and Western spiritual traditions and practices.

She loves being connected to the earth and the heavens on 22 acres in the middle of the forest overlooking the Tasman Sea and adopting a lifestyle that is completely off the grid, totally self-sufficient for water and electricity.

She is a globe-trotting entrepreneur with a passion for accumulating frequent flyer points on her travels.

www.ingramcontent.com/pod-product-compliance
Lightning Source LLC
Chambersburg PA
CBHW050311010526
44107CB00055B/2196